Marikana

MARIKANA
A View from the Mountain
and a Case to Answer

Peter Alexander
Luke Sinwell
Thapelo Lekgowa
Botsang Mmope
and
Bongani Xezwi

Cover photograph: A view from the mountain. Photograph taken from the top of the mountain on 15 August 2012. The area with trees is the hillock. Nkaneng informal settlement lies beyond, on the right near the top of the photograph. The pylons carry electricity to Lonmin, but none of this goes to the settlement. The area between the hillock and Nkaneng is the killing field, where the first deaths occurred on 16 August.

The following photographs are acknowledged and credited:
Greg Marinovich: front cover and p33
Peter Alexander: pp17 and 41
Reuters/The Bigger Picture: p37, bottom photo, and p149
Amandla magazine: p37, top and middle photos
Thapelo Lekgowa: pp49, 59, 63, 141 and 145
Asanda Benya: p55
Joseph Mathunjwa: p137

Marikana: A View from the Mountain and a Case to Answer
By Peter Alexander, Luke Sinwell, Thapelo Lekgowa,
Botsang Mmope and Bongani Xezwi
First published by Jacana Media, South Africa, in 2012
Published in the UK by Bookmarks Publications in 2013
Bookmarks Publications, 1 Bloomsbury Street, London WC1B 3QE
© Peter Alexander, Thapelo Lekgowa, Botsang Mmope,
Luke Sinwell and Bongani Xezwi, 2012
© Maps by John McCann
All rights reserved
ISBN 978 1 909026 25 4
Cover design Maggie Davey and Shawn Paikin
Printed by Russell Press

Contents

About the authors

PETER ALEXANDER is a professor of sociology at the University of Johannesburg and holds the South African Research Chair in Social Change. In the UK, he gained degrees from London University, was an academic at Oxford University, and held leadership positions in the Southern Africa Solidarity Campaign, Anti-Nazi League, Miners' Defence League and Socialist Workers Party. He moved permanently to South Africa in 1998. His interests include labour history, specifically Witbank miners, and community protests. He is a co-author of *Class in Soweto*, to be published by the University of KwaZulu-Natal Press at the beginning of 2013.

THAPELO LEKGOWA is a freelance research fieldworker working with the South African Research Chair in Social Change. After school he worked for a platinum mine. He is a full-time political activist, who learns and teaches on the street. A co-founder of the Che Guevara Film Club and a member of the Qinamsebemzi Collective, he is a member of the Marikana Support Committee.

BOTSANG MMOPE is a herbal healer associated with Green World Africa. Over the past seven years he has worked on various projects with the University of Johannesburg, including research on class, strikes and, recently, the Chair in Social Change's 'Rebellion of the Poor'. He is an active member of the Soweto Electricity Crisis Committee.

LUKE SINWELL is a Senior Researcher with the Research Chair in Social Change at the University of Johannesburg. He obtained a PhD in Development Studies from the University of the Witwatersrand in 2009. His interests include the politics and conceptualisation of participatory development and governance, direct action and action research. He is co-editor of *Contesting Transformation: Popular Resistance in Twenty-First-Century South Africa* published by Pluto Press at the end of 2012.

BONGANI XEZWI is a freelance research fieldworker who has done work on waste pickers, food production, police brutality and service delivery protests. Recently he conducted life history interviews for the book *Mining Faces*. He was Gauteng organiser of the Landless People's Movement and is currently the Gauteng organiser for the Right to Know Campaign.

Acknowledgements

Funding for our research has come from the Raith Foundation and from the South African Research Chair in Social Change, which is funded by the Department of Science and Technology, administered by the National Research Foundation and hosted by the Faculty of Humanities at the University of Johannesburg. We are grateful to Prof. Rory Ryan, Dean of Humanities, Prof. Lionel Posthumus, the faculty's Vice Dean for Research, and Lucinda Landen, the Research Chair's Administration Officer for supporting the project.

Interviews were translated by Bridget Ndibongo, Mbongisi Dyantyi, Andisiwe Nakani and the research fieldworkers. Mamatlwe Sebei helped us by conducting preliminary interviews. We also received assistance from Marcelle Dawson, Shannon Walsh, David Moore and Fox Pooe.

John McCann provided the maps, which add considerably to this book. We are also very grateful to Joseph Mathunjwa, Asanda Benya and Greg Marinovich who kindly provided photographs.

The book was peer reviewed, with the reviewers providing supportive reports and valuable advice. James Nichol and Rehad Desai also read and commented on parts of the manuscript, as did members of Peter Alexander's family. Encouraging feedback was received at lectures given in Johannesburg, Detroit, Oxford and London.

Staff at Jacana, especially the editor Maggie Davey, did a superb job, working under considerable time pressures.

Most of all we are grateful to the Marikana strikers and community members we interviewed. They assisted us despite trauma, the watchful eyes of the police, and sometimes hunger. We were also assisted by Joseph Mathunjwa and other leaders of the Association of Mineworkers and Construction Union, and we are indebted to them as well. Many of those we interviewed participated in a reference group, which helped us correct mistakes. Remaining errors of fact, interpretation and judgment are our own. We have conveyed the perspective of workers involved in the massacre to the best of our ability, and we hope they will feel that we have done them justice. We have done our best to be accurate and rigorous, but slips are possible in an enterprise of this kind and we apologise in advance for any we have made.

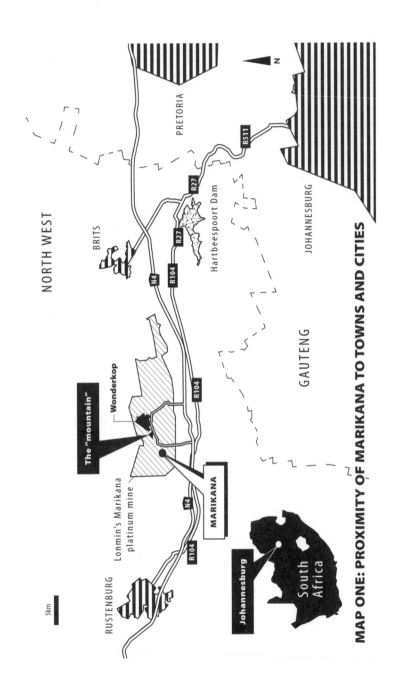

MAP ONE: PROXIMITY OF MARIKANA TO TOWNS AND CITIES

Marikana: A View from the Mountain and a Case to Answer

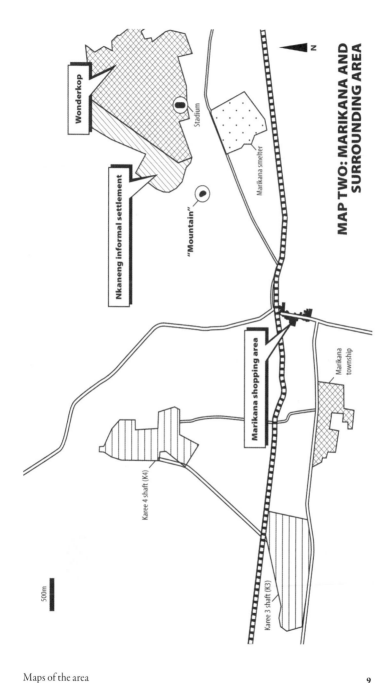

MAP TWO: MARIKANA AND SURROUNDING AREA

N

500m

Wonderkop

Nkaneng informal settlement

"Mountain"

Stadium

Marikana smelter

Marikana shopping area

Marikana township

Karee 4 shaft (K4)

Karee 3 shaft (K3)

Maps of the area

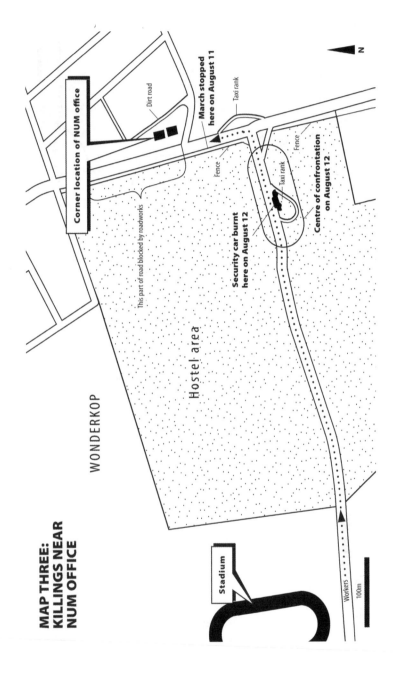

MAP THREE:
KILLINGS NEAR
NUM OFFICE

Corner location of NUM office

Dirt road

March stopped here on August 11

Taxi rank

Fence

This part of road blocked by roadworks

Fence

Taxi rank

Security car burnt here on August 12

Centre of confrontation on August 12

Fence

N

WONDERKOP

Hostel area

Stadium

Workers

100m

Marikana: A View from the Mountain and a Case to Answer

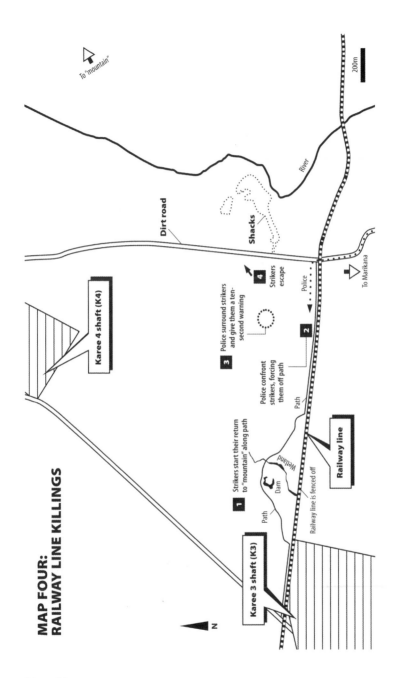

MAP FOUR: RAILWAY LINE KILLINGS

Karee 4 shaft (K4)

Karee 3 shaft (K3)

Dirt road

Shacks

River

To "mountain"

200m

Railway line

Railway line is fenced off

To Marikana

Police

Dam

Wetland

Path

Path

N

1 Strikers start their return to "mountain" along path

2 Police confront strikers, forcing them off path

3 Police surround strikers and give them a ten-second warning

4 Strikers escape

MAP FIVE:
SITE OF THE MASSACRE

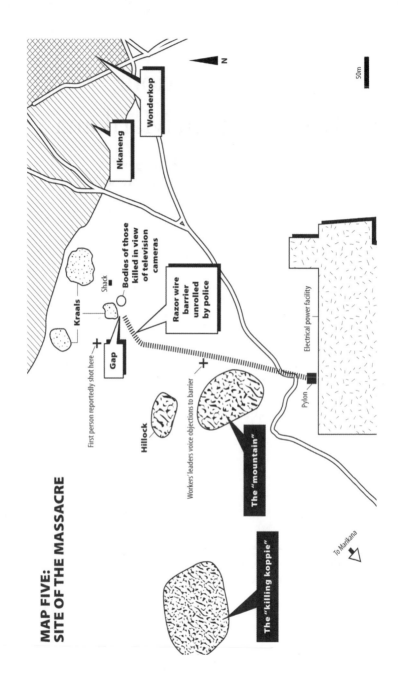

Introduction:
Encounters in Marikana

**Luke Sinwell, Thapelo Lekgowa,
Botsang Mmope and Bongani Xezwi**

On a blistering hot afternoon in Marikana just a few weeks after the brutal massacre of 16 August 2012, 10,000 striking workers carrying knobkerries and tall whips waited patiently in the sun. Four of us, researchers from the University of Johannesburg, found ourselves in the midst of the crowd. The mood was unclear, but seemed volatile. The workers were singing '*makuliwe*' [isiXhosa for 'let there be a fight']. We felt the force of the movement. One wrong move by the police could shift this peaceful moment into yet another bloody affair.

Following the massacre, workers had started moving in tight-knit battalions, using these formations to protect themselves, especially the strike's leaders. In what has become an emblemic feature of this workers' resistance movement, the group stopped and kneeled about 20 metres from the police vehicles. At this point five *madoda* [men] stepped forward to negotiate. As the workers explained, 'we can all sing, but we can't all speak at once'. The five madoda are the voices of the masses behind them, and they could be alternated at any time depending on negotiating capabilities and who they were speaking with. Their plan was to head for the smelter (where the platinum is processed and refined) demanding that it shut down its operations. At this stage, 95 per cent of workers at Lonmin, the third largest platinum mine in the world, were on strike. The smelter was the only unit still operating and the marchers wanted the workers there to join the strike.

Marikana was in effect witnessing an undeclared state of emergency. Police and Lonmin were on one side, and the workers were on the other. Over the next week, a thousand troops were deployed and orders were given by the police that people must stay off the streets. On this particular day, 12 September, the carloads of local and international media that had been camping out at the scene sped off quickly. It seemed like an evacuation. We wondered if we were in the wrong place at the wrong time. Two of us thought it was unsafe and wanted to flee; the other two felt we should stay and observe. In the end we didn't have much choice. Suddenly the mass of workers kneeled to the ground. There was no space to drive our car away, so we too kneeled down. We learned later from the workers that this was to ensure a calm and quiet environment for the five madodas' negotiations. The workers were also very cautious. They crouched with their weapons down and to their side, as they did on 16 August when they were attacked. At the same time, they were ready to pick them up and fight, but only if it was necessary to defend themselves.

There was no academic training that could have prepared us for our experiences that day, or for others that came before and after. Each one offered us new challenges as researchers and, more importantly, as human beings. As we learned more about this merciless and bloody massacre through the workers' voices and eye-witness accounts, we came to the realisation that this was not only preventable, it had been planned in advance. In contrast to the dominant view put forth by the media, government and the National Union of Mineworkers (NUM), which suggests that the workers were an unruly and dangerous mob who needed to be controlled and contained, we learned that the workers were, and remain, disciplined, peaceful and very well organised. The consciousness of South Africans and others has been scarred by media footage that makes it seem like strikers were charging the police, and defending themselves against savages. As several of the eye-witness accounts of workers who were on the mountain during the massacre testify, and as Peter Alexander recounts, workers were not on the offensive, but were literally running for their lives on 16 August. Some were even shot in the back or in the back of the head while running away.

This is the first book that attempts to understand the massacre on 16 August. It can only provide a starting point for future scholarship and it does not attempt to explain what happened from the perspective of all stakeholders involved. Moreover, when framing the raw interviews that follow, we have extended beyond superficial journalistic accounts, probing into the experiences and lives of the miners. This has only been possible because of a concern to build relationships of trust in a tumultuous, albeit very short, period of time. Too often, researchers go into a locality in order to obtain information from respondents but have limited commitment and never return. This can create a situation in which locals are sceptical of future researchers and refuse to share what they know. We have sustained relationships with many of the workers and have, in small but certain ways, acted in solidarity with them. Of course it would be naïve to assume that this limited engagement over only a few months could produce ethnographic depth, but we hope that it will be the start of a longer engagement.

While the primary focus of our research and interviews was the men who were on the mountain, our most hard-hitting and heart-wrenching experiences were often with the family members, wives and children of the victims. Interviews and other forms of research can take an emotional toll both on the respondent and on the researchers. For Thapelo and Luke, our most painful experience was visiting the families of the deceased in the Eastern Cape, where we began creating biographies of the 34 men who were killed. We attended two funerals and visited seven families in total; entering hut upon hut, seeing family upon family in their rural villages in the poorest province of South Africa, from which most of the workers have migrated. The families were in their mourning period, but still they opened their hearts to us.

We watched six young children playing—none of them had any idea that their father was dead. Rather, as is the tradition, they were told 'Daddy won't be coming home anymore'. It is only later in life that they will learn that their father was killed by police for the 'crime' of fighting for his right to a better life. To these children things were just normal. We felt helpless when the families asked us for immediate help. People poured out their problems and told us what the solution might be, hoping that we would pass on the message to the powers that be. The words are still haunting us: 'Go ask government and Lonmin who will be feeding these kids.'

We stayed late one night in Marikana West, the township where many workers live. Bongani and Luke were interviewing one of the workers who had been arrested on 16 August, but he did not want to give us information without the approval of his lawyer. He asked us to walk, through the dark and empty streets, to his home where he had the business card of his lawyer. When we arrived we realised that he was a backyard dweller who was staying in a tiny zinc shack. As we were about to get to his door his wife came out, very distressed, and stated quietly but firmly and in an angry tone: 'My brothers, get inside! I want to know why are you here?' As we went inside she demanded proof of our identities. She then explained:

> I am asking because there are people around our area who call themselves researchers. Who come to our houses and take our husbands for an interview. And that will be the end of us seeing our husbands. That thing happened in Bop [Western Platinum] Mine when a husband was taken by interviewers and he was never found.

We tried to explain the purpose of our research and why we were in Marikana. We showed them our University of Johannesburg identity cards. After a few minutes she became calmer and accepted our purpose. As we walked out of the shack we became really aware of the tension the community was dealing with. No one felt safe and people believed that outsiders could even kidnap and kill their loved ones. This was the environment of post-massacre Marikana. We decided to avoid speaking to people at night as much as possible, both because we feared for our own safety and because we did not want to make residents feel more uncomfortable.

Late in the afternoon, Botsang entered Nkaneng, an informal settlement in Marikana from which one can see the mountain where the workers were killed. What follows was remembered clearly: I felt uneasy and I shivered. I had never walked in that settlement alone and I did not know how the people there would react to me. It seemed as if everyone was looking at me, and with my yellow University of

A shack in Nkaneng informal settlement, which provides a home for many mineworkers and their families.

Johannesburg bag, they could tell that I was a stranger. I was taken by a man into a one-room shack where a woman, a widow of one of the mineworkers killed on 16 August, sat on the bed. One young girl was in the room making tea. That one room was used for sleeping, as a living room, for bathing and for cooking.

The widow and I were left alone and I explained to her the purpose of the research we were doing—so that the next generation could understand what happened during the massacre. She began to open up. I asked her if her husband had ever discussed what happened during the strike. She explained that her husband was earning about R4,000 before he passed away. Her husband's back, she said, had been full of scars. He was a rock drill operator (RDO), the group that initially led the strike in Lonmin, and the rocks would fall on his back, injuring him. She recounted that on 16 August he was arrested and murdered by the police while he was on strike with others fighting for better pay. The family found him in a mortuary in Rustenburg. It looked as though his skull had been slashed with something like a panga, and the mortuary refused her and the family entry when they wanted to see the rest of the body. She then asked me:

> Actually, who ordered the police to kill our husbands, was it Lonmin? Or, was it the government that signed that the police must kill our husbands? Today I am called a widow and my children are called fatherless because of the police. I blame the mine, the police and the government because they are the ones who control this country.

I then proceeded to ask her about the future of her children and she responded:

> Our future is no more and I feel very hopeless because I do not know who will educate my children. My husband never made us suffer. He was always providing for us. The government has promised us that they will support us for three months with groceries, but they only gave us three things: 12.5 kg of mealie meal, 12.5 kg of flour and 12.5 kg of samp. That's it. My husband was sending us money every month and we had enough to eat. Now the mine has killed him. The children of the police who killed him eat bread and eggs every morning while my children eat pap with tea.

Her family consists of six children, five of whom are in school while one is looking for work. The other day, the younger son was asking his older sister: 'Why is Daddy not coming home?' He had heard that his father and others were fighting with the police at the foot of the mountain. 'Where is he?' he inquired further. A nine-year-old girl asked her [mother], 'Mommy, why are the police killing Daddy, while we are still so young?'

The above encounters highlight that we did not go to Marikana untouched by people's experiences with life, death and struggle. The neutral researcher who is detached or not affected by his or her own positionality and perceptions of what is taking place is an illusion. The call to end the strikes and the statement that the workers were threatening the economy or the value of the rand, something we read in the newspapers every day, are providing one story. There is another, that, when compared with their bosses, the workers deserve R12,500, which was their demand, and that they were brutally murdered in the interests of capitalist labour relations of production. While the former ignores the structural and actual living and working conditions of the miners, the latter has received virtually no attention in mainstream analyses.

Perhaps nowhere has the conflict between working-class power and capitalist interests been more acute, and rarely has it spilled more blood. The Marikana Judicial Commission of Inquiry, launched on 1 October 2012 without the knowledge of the families or victims, and with very few workers actually present, may conclude otherwise. It aims to provide 'truth and justice' on the basis of evidence presented to the commissioners, but it has not observed working conditions underground and operates in a courtroom environment alienating for ordinary people. In fact, key leaders of the workers' committee have been arrested, intimidated and tortured during the time in which the commission has taken place, and we therefore question the extent to which the commission is able to provide a space that is not biased against the workers' perspective. One of the main aims of this book is to fill this gap. Whatever the official conclusion, we maintain that Marikana was not just a human tragedy, but rather a sober undertaking by powerful agents of the state and capital who consciously organised to kill workers who had temporarily stopped going underground in order to extract the world's most precious metal—platinum.

But not all has been bleak. While we have been saddened, we have also been inspired. The strike at Lonmin symbolised, as much as ever, raw working-class power—unhindered by the tenets of existing collective bargaining and middle-class politics. The workers developed their own class analysis of the situation at Lonmin and, instead of being silenced and falling back when the steel arm of the state mowed down 34 of their colleagues, they became further determined, and more workers united until all of Lonmin came to a standstill.

Workers realised that NUM was too close to the bosses and obstructed their struggle, and that the other union involved, the Association of Mineworkers and Construction Union (AMCU), lacked the formal bargaining rights that could advance their demands.

In order to be strong, they needed to unite amongst themselves. There had been earlier meetings of representatives from the various shafts, but it was the first general meeting, held on 9 August, that brought together all Lonmin's RDOs in order to formulate a memorandum that reflected the demands of the entire work population—for a salary of R12,500. An independent workers' committee was elected representing the three segments of Lonmin—Eastern, Western and Karee—and it became directly accountable to the workers.

The leaders were elected on the basis of their historical leadership in recreational spaces, the community and the workplace. Mambush, or 'the man in the green blanket', one of the leaders who was killed during the massacre, had obtained his nickname from a Sundowns' soccer player named 'Mambush Mudau'. He was chosen since he had organised soccer games and always resolved minor problems in the workplace. He was particularly well known for having a mild temperament and for his conflict-resolution skills both at the workplace and at his home in the Eastern Cape. Others were chosen because they had previously dealt with emergencies that had occurred in the communities where the miners had originated, including the Eastern Cape, Lesotho, Swaziland, Mozambique and elsewhere. When someone passes away in Wonderkop, workers often show their leadership by taking responsibility for the process of alerting the family of the miner and organising to ensure that the body gets to the respective home and that miners are transported to the funeral. They also manage and collect donations from co-workers to give to the family of the deceased. The workers' committee was reconstituted several times—some gave up, others were killed, while some remained on the committee from its inception on 9 August until after the strike.

This workers' agency and leadership is no obscure radical rhetoric or theory of ivory tower academics or non-governmental organisations (NGOs). Rather, it is the unfettered praxis of the working class—which could not be contained, even with national security, the ANC, NUM, and the ideology of the ruling class pitted against it. This book provides a history from below—a story of ordinary people who had previously been relegated to the margins of society. Here, we acknowledge them for their involvement in the strike and for their

Marikana: A View from the Mountain and a Case to Answer

bravery during an extraordinary and tragic moment in time. The pain of the workers seeps through their stories. It is tangible, sometimes gut-wrenching. We hope you can understand the massacre through the lens of the victims, those who continue to mourn the deaths of their loved ones and colleagues.

In the core of the book, we let the Marikana workers speak for themselves. NUM leaders deny certain of the testimonies given. We undertook more than 30 formal interviews, joined workers' and community representatives for their meetings, participated in protests, and engaged in countless unrecorded conversations. Finally, we were privileged to be able to meet with a reference group of 14 strikers, many of them part of the leadership, six representatives from the community and two AMCU leaders. We included interviews in this book that are largely representative of the workers' voices. The interviews that we excluded do not challenge the narrative put forward in the book. Rather, they tend to confirm it.

A large number of the interviews were conducted under the mountain, where workers held meetings in the open air, others were on the streets and some were in people's homes. Some of the interviews contain material that deals with personal biographies of mineworkers in order to help the reader to understand how and why they came to Marikana. We do not draw this out extensively, but rather allow the readers to form their own impressions.

In the beginning we engaged with almost anybody prepared to talk with us, but later were able to interview leaders of the strike. The people we interviewed stood a very real chance of being victimised by the police or Lonmin, so we have made them anonymous. Anonymity was an undertaking made to our interviewees, and it is one that perhaps contributed to gaining testimony unvarnished by public exposure. For the most part our research was completed before lawyers started taking statements, at which point narratives may have become formalised and less spontaneous. We do not know of previous academic interviews gained so soon after a massacre, and we hope that this contributes to the unique character of the volume.

For the book, space constraints compelled us to make a selection from our main interviews. These are preceded by three background interviews. The first of these is with the president of AMCU, a union that sympathised with the strikers and to which many of them belonged. We think the interview is important because the union's voice has been under-represented and widely misrepresented in the media, sometimes maliciously so. A second interview is with an RDO, who talks about his job, and a third is with a miner's wife. We then include sections of three speeches given in the days immediately after the massacre; the first two by strike leaders, the third by the general secretary of AMCU. Ten interviews with mineworkers follow the speeches.

Before the interviews and speeches, there is a narrative account of events leading up to the massacre. The five maps at the start of the book provide a chronological and geographical framework that assists with locating the voices that follow, and the section draws mainly on the interviews, which are extensively quoted. The reference group enabled us to correct important details, but any mistakes are ours and ours alone, and we apologise, to the workers especially, for any errors. The narrative is the beginning of a history from below, and will be expanded and modified by evidence presented to the inquiry (which will be valuable even if the commission interprets it in ways with which we and the workers disagree). Our main aim in this book has been to indicate what happened, and offer proximate explanations. A deeper history providing a better account of motivations and sociology will require, in particular, attention to life history. In the analysis and conclusion to the book we contextualise the massacre to propose a preliminary assessment of its wider significance.

We hope that by the end of the book the reader will have a clearer understanding of what happened in Marikana and why. We hope that you will share with us a sense of the strain and pain of the miners' lives and labour, the bravery of their struggle, the cruelty tied to their boss's drive for capacious profits, the corruption of NUM and, most awful of all, the unnecessary police brutality that resulted in the largest state massacre of South African citizens since the Soweto Uprising of 1976.

2

The massacre:
A narrative account based on
workers' testimonies

Peter Alexander

On 16 August 2012 the South African police massacred 34 strikers participating in a peaceful gathering on public land outside the small town of Marikana. The workers' demand was simple. They wanted their employer, Lonmin, to listen to their case for a decent wage. But this threatened a system of labour relations that had boosted profits for Lonmin, and had protected the privileges of the dominant union, the National Union of Mineworkers (NUM). It was decided to deploy 'maximum force' against the workers. Our narrative includes brief accounts of events prior to 16 August, when ten people died, and offers insights into why workers were prepared to die for their cause. It draws mainly on interviews with strikers conducted in the six weeks following the event, and a selection of this testimony appears later in the book.

Some background to the strike

Poverty drove our interviewees to work at Lonmin, and fear of losing their jobs means they tolerate some of the most arduous and dangerous working conditions imaginable. The second background interview in this book provides a glimpse of work undertaken by rock drill operators (RDOs), the category of employees who led the strike. Other underground workers also perform heavy manual work, often doubled up, under the threat of rock falls and machinery accidents. Making matters worse, the air underground is 'artificial' and full of dust and chemicals. TB is widespread and illness is common. Of course there are safety regulations, but according to Mineworker 8, who was qualified as a safety officer: 'We work under a lot of pressure from our bosses because they want production, and then there is also intimidation. They want you to do things that are sub-standard, and if you don't want to do that and follow the rules... they say they will fire you or beat you, things like that.'[1] He recalled a worker who had lost his leg because he had been forced, through threat of a 'charge', to work in a dangerous place. Peer pressure, too, is a factor. Mineworker 7, a woman, told us: 'When you start saying "safety, safety, safety", they say "What should we do? Should we not take out the *stof* [blasted ore-bearing rock], and just sit here, because you don't want to be hurt?"'. For the Marikana strikers, the fear of death, present on 16 August, was not a new experience.

In South Africa, a typical working day lasts eight hours, but Lonmin workers we spoke to said they could not 'knock off' until they had reached their target, which often meant working 12 hours, sometimes more (Mineworker 8 mentioned working a 15-hour shift). Mineworker 7 complained: 'They do not even give you time to eat lunch. They just say your lunch box must remain on the surface'. Referring to incessant pressure to reach targets, Mineworker 5 protested that 'conditions in the mines are those of oppression'. Moreover, it is taken for granted that mine labour also involves anti-social hours, with shifts starting at 05:30 or 21:00 and Saturday-working being a requirement. A group of wives that I spoke with agreed in chorus that their husbands always returned home exhausted. My sense is that today's Lonmin workers often slave for more hours a week than the 1920s colliery workers I studied, and they probably work harder.[2]

What does a worker get paid for such hazardous and strenuous work? With few exceptions, those we spoke to said they received between R4,000 and R5,000 per month. These were 'take home' figures, and included, so we were told, a standard housing, or 'living out', allowance.[3] Figures vary and calculations are affected by exchange rates, but miners in Australia and the UK can expect to earn ten times this amount. Workers complained that bonuses and overtime payments were negligible. General assistants claimed they received under R4,000 and a supervisor said he received a little more than R5,000. Such money goes quickly, especially if it is necessary to remit funds to family members who are unemployed, which is common. Major expenditure includes rent for a shack (about R450), food (with prices rising rapidly), school and medical expenses, and interest on loans.[4] The inequality accompanying low pay provides added anguish. For instance, Mineworker 4 observed: 'You will hear that stocks are up, but we get nothing'. Highlighting the continuing salience of 'race', he added: 'The white people reprimand us if we do not do our work properly or make a mistake. It would have been better to be reprimanded knowing that we were getting pay'.

Several workers had long-standing gripes about their union, NUM, for its failure to support them over critical issues, such as safety and pay. Mineworker 8 claimed that 'NUM, truly speaking, it always sides with the employer.' He added: 'When a person gets hurt here underground, the employer and NUM change the story. They say: "that person got hurt in his shack".' Another worker, Mineworker 4, complained: 'We have been struggling while the union leaders were comfortable, drinking tea. When they have a problem, the management helps them quickly. Even their cellphones are always loaded with airtime, R700, R800'.

Matters came to a head at the end of May 2011, following NUM's suspension of its popular branch chairperson at Karee, one of Lonmin's three mines at Marikana. Mineworker 8 provides an account of events. According to him, members 'loved' the chairperson, Steve, because he refused to take bribes from management and 'he always came with straight things... things that NUM never wanted us to know'.[5] The suspension followed a dispute about a payout from a trust fund established to enable workers to benefit from profits made over the preceding five years. The workers responded to Steve's suspension by engaging in an unprotected strike. After a week, NUM intervened. Some activists believe the effect of its action was interpreted as a sanction to dismiss the whole Karee labour force, 9,000 workers.[6] Whilst this was a set-back for the workers, nearly all of them were re-hired.

According to Mineworker 8, for the next three months 'the situation was bad'. He then explained: 'It was very bad because if you do not have a union the employer can do whatever he likes to you'. Nevertheless, workers continued to meet in a semi-clandestine manner, with individuals anonymously convening meetings by pinning a 'paper' on a notice board. Even though NUM had been discredited, some workers considered bringing it back, believing that any union would be better than none. However, the majority were opposed to this scenario, and it was at this point that most of the Karee workers went over to the Association of Mineworkers and Construction Union (AMCU). By early 2012, AMCU had gained representation rights at Karee, had won some support at Eastern Mine (often referred to as Bop Mine, its old name) and had a few people at Western Mine.[7] AMCU's presence at Marikana is, then, a recent phenomenon, and, as with the union's formation back in 2001, the catalyst was NUM's suspension of a popular leader.[8]

By July 2012 there was widespread dissatisfaction over pay[9]. This was particularly acute among RDOs at Karee Mine, who complained that, since they had to work without an assistant (unlike their counterparts at Eastern and Western), they were doing two jobs, and should be remunerated accordingly. The implication was that their pay should be raised from about R4,000 per month, to about R7,500.[10] Following a mass protest at Karee on 1 August, the manager there awarded his RDOs a bonus of R750 per month.[11] Elsewhere, RDOs working with an assistant received an extra R500 and assistants got an additional R250. Now, nobody was happy. The Karee men still felt underpaid and RDOs on other mines wanted the same higher increase.[12] To add to the mix, the Karee RDOs had secured a partial victory without involving NUM, thus boosting their confidence while antagonising the NUM leadership. With RDOs now protesting at different shafts, management took the view that their demands should be directed towards the central Lonmin management.[13] This provided added stimulus to co-ordinated action, and by 6 August representatives from across the company had established an informal committee. This body then convened a meeting for all Lonmin RDOs.

The strike starts

The assembly took place on Thursday 9 August, Women's Day, a public holiday, at Wonderkop Stadium (see Map 2). At a rally held two days after the massacre, one of the leaders, Tholakele Dlunga (known as Bhele) narrated as follows: 'For those of you who do not know, this started on the ninth, when workers of Lonmin gathered to try and address the issue of wage dissatisfaction... to try get our heads together and find a way forward.'[14]. Various demands were being raised, and it was agreed that there should be a common proposal for R12,500 per month.[15] However, the objective was to secure a decent increase, and the specific figure was seen as a negotiating position. Mineworker 1 expressed himself thus: 'Yes, we demanded 12.5 but we... only wanted to talk. We wanted management to negotiate that maybe at the end we will get around 8.9'. NUM was not advancing workers' claims for better remuneration, and the big problem was getting Lonmin to talk directly with the workers. For Mineworker 1 the thinking was: 'We will go to the employer on our own and ask for that money... we will go to the employer ourselves because the work we do there is very hard and is killing us.' The practical conclusion was that workers would deliver their demand to the management the following day.

The meeting brought together workers from across Marikana and it elected a committee that reflected the diversity of the workforce. According to one source, the original committee included two workers from the Western shafts, three from the Eastern shafts and three from those in Karee.[16] NUM was still the dominant force in Western and Eastern while AMCU prevailed in Karee, but union affiliation was not the issue. Another worker recalled that the committee was 'representative of all cultural constituencies. It had to be made up of people coming from different provinces'.[17] Women were not represented, however. According to Mineworker 7, a woman, this was because they were more vulnerable to victimisation by the employer—because there were fewer of them, so more obvious. Responding to the question 'If they were not afraid they would have been elected?' she said: 'They would have been nicely elected'.[18] Later on, the committee was expanded, and included people who had responsibility for organising the funerals and for welcoming and providing information for visitors.[19] Significantly, a key responsibility of the original committee was, as Mineworker 3 put it, its ability to maintain 'peace and order'. He argued: '[In] other strikes, people mess up and damage stores and beat people, things like that. So those people [the committee] were able to control people.' Mineworker 1 added that, in electing the committee, workers 'wanted to make sure there was order'. In light of subsequent events, this commitment to peace and order, embodied in the leadership of the strike, is highly pertinent. As we will see, the workers were prepared to defend themselves, but they did not initiate violence.

The main decision of the meeting was that the following day, 10 August, the RDOs would strike. At this stage other employees were expected to work normally, though, in reality, without the RDOs production would be minimal.[20] The strikers marched to the offices of Lonmin's local senior management, located at the so-called 'LPD' (Lonmin Platinum Division). They were met by a white security officer who said the managers would respond in 15 minutes. But there was no response, and after waiting for three hours the workers' leaders pressed the matter, only to be informed that their demands had to be channelled through NUM.[21] Had the management met the protesting RDOs, the deaths that followed could have been averted, but NUM opposed this course of action.[22] Mineworker 10 used the language of paternalism to express his frustration: 'We blame the employer for not caring about us, because as a parent, as a head office, if there is a dispute in the family he will go and address it, find out what is the problem, so that his children will lay their hearts on the table [and] tell him "this is our problem"'.

Rebuffed, the protesters returned to the stadium. There they agreed that the strike should be expanded to include other workers, starting with the night shift. They also convened a meeting of all workers, to be held at the stadium the following morning.

The NUM shootings

That next morning, 11 August, the meeting agreed to follow management's instruction and put their case to NUM. Some of the workers justified this decision in terms of correct protocol. Mineworker 1, for instance, told us: 'We decided to go to the NUM offices so that they can tell us what we should do now, because we went to the employer on our own and they [NUM] went and stopped us from talking to the employer, and we wanted them to tell us what to do.' Mineworker 10 put the matter this way: 'We acknowledged that we made a mistake, that even though we did not want them [NUM] to represent us, we should have at least informed them that we were going to approach the employer'. Bhele said: 'We admitted that we took a wrong turn'.[23] The strikers marched in the direction of the NUM office, located less than a kilometre away in the centre of Wonderkop. It is important to note that they were not armed, not even with traditional weapons. According to Mineworker 10, 'We were singing, and no one was holding any weapon'. In answer to the question, 'did you have your weapons then?', Mineworker 8 responded: 'No we did not have our weapons on that day.'

After passing the mine hostels, strikers turned left towards the NUM office (see Map 3)[24]. But they never reached their destination. Before them, at a point where the main road ahead was under construction, there was a line of armed men wearing red T-shirts. The strikers halted their march close to the main taxi rank to the right. The armed men opened fire. The strikers scattered, mostly in the direction from where they had come. But two men were left behind, badly injured. According to contributors in our Reference Group discussion, one of these managed to clamber over the fence that separates the road from the hostels, and was able to escape. The second man got as far as the smaller taxi rank just inside the hostel grounds, where he allegedly died (see Map 3).[25]

Jared Sacks researched the event, concluding: 'Once striking RDOs were about 100–150 metres away from the NUM office, eye-witnesses, both participants in the march and informal traders in and around a nearby taxi rank, reported without exception that the "top five" NUM leaders and other shop stewards, between 15 and 20 in all, came out of the office and began shooting at the protesting strikers'.[26] The implication is that the men in red T-shirts included some of NUM's local leadership. Apparently security guards were also present, but fired their guns into the air.[27] Sacks' account was corroborated by the testimony we collected. None of the workers who described the scene doubted that the gunmen were from NUM. Mineworker 8 stated: 'When we were near the offices we found them outside, those people, our leaders, I can put it like that, they came out. Our leaders came out of the offices already having guns, and they just came out shooting'. Mineworker 4's account is similar: 'We were not fighting them. They [NUM] were the ones who shot at us… It was the union leaders, the union committee. They were the ones who shot at us.' Mineworker 9 provided an interpretation: 'They [NUM comrades] started shooting at us… It became clear that we were not accepted by the very union we voted for, and it also showed that they had strong relationships with our employers'. Similarly, Mineworker 8 concluded: 'They [NUM leadership] don't want us getting the money and I am very sure of that… because they are the ones who are always standing with management.' Mineworker 10 was shocked by NUM's response: 'When the NUM saw us approaching its offices it didn't even ask, it just opened bullets on the workers,' he said, adding: 'We thought, as its members, it would welcome us and hear what we had to say, and criticise us, because it had the right to criticise us after we went over its head'.

In a submission to the Farlam Commission, Karel Tip, acting on behalf of the NUM, accepted that some of the union's members used firearms. He did not acknowledge that NUM bullets killed any strikers, and the bodies of slain miners have not been recovered, nor did he mention that anyone was hurt. Two men were, however, seriously injured and hospitalised. It now seems likely that the two strikers who were shot did not die, but it is understandable that many workers thought that this was indeed the case.[28] From our interviewees and our Reference Group, it is clear that many, probably most, of the people that were being attacked, including the man who allegedly died, were in fact NUM's own members. NUM leaders robustly deny they would have consciously shot at strikers, including their own members. But certainly some workers believed this.

In any case, the event was a turning point. Workers fled from the scene and headed towards the stadium. But security guards refused them re-entry, threatening to use force if necessary. The workers then headed for Wonderkop Koppie, the so-called 'mountain', two kilometres further west. This would be their home for the next five nights and days, though, of course, they did not know this at the time. One advantage of staying on the mountain is that it provided a good view. According to Mineworker 9, 'The mountain is high [and] we chose it deliberately after NUM killed our members, so that we could easily see people when they come'. Though some workers went home at night, he and Mineworker 8 both refused to do so, because they had a fear of being killed (probably by NUM). Mineworker 8 described life on the mountain: 'We were singing, talking and sharing ideas, and encouraging each other, that here is not the same as your house, and one has to be strong... You are just sitting here, and making fire and putting money together'. Mineworker 9 added: 'We were helped by the people in the nearby shacks who brought us food'.

It was only at this point, after the shooting of their comrades, that workers gathered their traditional weapons. Mineworker 8 responded to the question 'So it was NUM that pushed you into carrying weapons?' with: 'Yes, because they shot at us and we were afraid that they will come back. We do not have guns, and so we thought it will be better that we have our traditional weapons.' Mineworker 1 provided valuable insight on the issue. 'My brother', he began, 'what I can say about the... spears and sticks [is] that we came with [them] from back home. It is our culture as black men, as Xhosa men... Even here... when I go look at anything... at night [such as the cows]... I always have my spear or stick... or when I have to go urinate, because I don't urinate in the house... I take my stick'. Then he added: 'A white man carries his gun when he leaves his house, that is how he was taught, and so sticks and spears that is the black man's culture'.

Further killings

On the Sunday, 12 August, workers went again to remonstrate with NUM officials. We can assume that this time they were carrying their weapons. Beyond the stadium, inside the hostel area, they were stopped by mine security (who included two '*boers*') and 'government police' who had a Hippo with them.[29] According to Mineworker 4: 'The mine security guards shot at us. But we did not go back. We kept going forward.' From subsequent conversations with workers we learned that two security men were dragged from their cars and killed with pangas or spears. Their cars were later set ablaze, and we saw the remains of one of these, which was located on a corner by the small taxi rank inside the hostel area. These new killings occurred close to where the striker had allegedly died the day before (see Map 3).

Monday, 13 August, was another day of bloodshed. Early in the morning, strikers received information that work was being undertaken at Karee No. 3 shaft (known as K3). Since this was the first full day of the strike it was not surprising that there was an element of scabbing, and a relatively small contingent was despatched to explain to the workers that they were expected to join the action. Accounts of the size of this 'flying picket' (to use a term from the UK) vary from under 30 to about a 100. See Map 2 (this shows that the entire journey would have been about 20 kilometres). Mineworker 2 provides a detailed account that is corroborated in other interviews and by versions we received from workers *in loco*. At K3 the deputation spoke with security guards, who said that, while they would look into the matter, as far as they knew nobody was working. According to the workers, the guards told them that rather than returning to the mountain via the K3 hostel and Marikana, which would have been the easier route, they should take paths across the veld (mostly flattish rough ground with occasional thorn trees and other shrubs). For the hike back to the mountain the group may have grown a little, but all our informants placed its size at under 200 people.

At first the route follows a dirt track alongside a railway line. After a detour around a small wetland, the workers found their way blocked by a well-armed detachment of police that had crossed the railway line on a small dirt road and turned left onto the track (see Map 4). The precise size of the police contingent is unclear, with Mineworker 2 saying the police included 'maybe three Hippos and plus/minus 20 vans' and a Reference Group contributor specifying about 14 Hippos but not mentioning vans (possibly treating armoured police 'vans' as 'Hippos'). The police forced the workers

Workers' leaders negotiating with the police on the afternoon of
15 August 2012.

off the path and encircled them (with a line of police stretched out
along the railway line). The response, it seems, came from Mambush,
later famous as 'the man in the green blanket' and probably the
most respected of the workers' leaders. He is reported to have said
that, while they were not refusing to give up their weapons, they
would only do so once they reached the safety of the mountain.
Mineworker 2 recounts that a Zulu-speaking policeman then warned
that he would count to ten, and if they had not conceded by then he
would give the order to fire. After the counting had started the workers began singing and moved off together towards the weakest point
in the police line, which was probably to the north-east, the direction of the mountain. At first the police gave way but, according to
Mineworker 2, after about ten metres they started shooting. In the
commotion that followed, three strikers (or two strikers and a local
resident) and two police officers were killed.[30] One of the strikers and
two of the police were killed to the west of the dirt road that crosses
the railway line (see Map 4). There is a suggestion that one of the

police may have been shot, accidentally, by another police officer.[31] On the other side of the road, a wounded civilian was hidden inside, or next to, a shack, but this was noticed by the police, who pursued him and then shot him several times at close range. The fifth fatality occurred north of the shack and to the east of the river (see Map 4). This worker was clearly fleeing.

Failed negotiations

On Tuesday, 14 August, a police negotiator arrived, accompanied by numerous Hippos. He was a white man, but addressed the workers in Fanakalo, which was regarded as novel for a white policeman.[31] He said that he came in peace, in friendship, and just wanted 'to build a relationship' (a formulation used in a number of interviews). He requested that the workers send five representatives to talk to him. This was the origin of the five madodas (Mineworker 3). This literally means 'five men', but it sometimes carries the connotation of self-selected or traditional leadership, thus implying a certain 'backwardness', in contrast to trade unions. In reality, as we have seen, the workers operated through an elected and representative workers' committee, one typical of well-organised modern strikes. Nevertheless, the strikers selected five representatives, and sent them to talk to the negotiator. Mineworker 3 provides a detailed account of proceedings. The representatives claimed that the negotiator and his team refused to leave the Hippo and speak to them on the same level, face to face. They also refused to provide their names, which was disconcerting to the workers, and at some point, later on, an *amadoda* tried to take a photograph of the police on a cellphone, but this was stopped. A worker who was part of the delegation claimed that one of the senior police was a white woman and that a company representative was also sitting in the Hippo. This was denied by the police.[33]

Nevertheless, the five madodas conveyed the view that all they wanted was to talk with their employer. They wanted him to come to the mountain, but, if necessary, they would go to him. The police departed, leaving workers with the impression that they would inform the employer of their request. However, when they returned

Marikana: A View from the Mountain and a Case to Answer

the next day, Wednesday, 15 August, it was without a representative of the employer.[34] Lonmin was refusing to talk to its striking workers. According to a strike leader, only three of the five madoda would survive the massacre that was imminent).[35]

Later on Wednesday, towards sunset, Senzeni Zokwana, president of NUM, arrived in a Hippo. Mineworker 10 complained that: 'We didn't see him, we were just informed to listen to our leader.' Mineworker 1 concurred: 'He was not in a right place to talk to us as a leader, as our president, this thing of him talking to us while he is in a Hippo. We wanted him to talk to us straight if he wanted to.' When he did speak, his message was simple, crude even. 'Mr Zokwana said the only thing he came to tell us was that he wanted us to go back to work, and that there was nothing else he was going to talk to us about'.[36] Apparently the workers repeated their demand that they only wanted their employer to address them, not Zokwana.[37] About five minutes after Zokwana left, Joseph Mathunjwa, president of AMCU, arrived, and although he was accompanied by a Hippo, he came in his own car.[38] According to Mineworker 6, Mathunjwa said that he was sympathetic to the strikers, but cautioned them that he too had been denied access to the employers. However, he added that because he had members at Karee he would try again to meet them the following day.

The police presence had increased on the Wednesday, and on the Thursday morning, 16 August, more forces arrived. This time the police were accompanied by 'soldiers', probably para-military police dressed in similar uniform to soldiers. Trailers carrying razor wire (which the workers mostly refer to as barbed wire) also arrived.[39] Mineworker 9 says that workers 'shouted' for other workers to join them. In the early afternoon on this fateful day, Mathunjwa returned, this time without any escort.[40] According to Mineworker 10, he told his audience that the employer never 'pitched' for their scheduled meeting, using the excuse that he was at another gathering (presumably with police chiefs).[41] Mineworker 10 added that Mathunjwa told the strikers they should return to work, because if they stayed on the mountain any longer a lot of people might die. There was some scepticism about this advice. For instance, Mineworker 2's response was that

Mathunjwa should 'go back, because we are not AMCU members, we are NUM members'. Mineworker 8's response was that, on the mountain, they had been eating together and making fire together, and it was like home. They weren't leaving, he said, adding that 'we do not want any union here'. Mineworker 9's account was slightly different again. According to him: 'We said, Comrade, go home. You did your best, but we will not leave here until we get the R12,500 we are requesting, and if we die fighting, so be it.' The last phrase resonated with a famous speech by Nelson Mandela, and Mineworker 9 pursued this, albeit with a twist. He said: 'We should talk and negotiate through striking, that is how Mandela fought for his country.' Mathunjwa made one last attempt to convince the workers. He went down on his knees and begged them to leave.[42] Few accepted his plea. Twenty minutes later the massacre began.

The massacre of 16 August 2012

There are photographs of the assembled workers when Mathunjwa was addressing them, just before he left the scene (see book cover for example). They are a large crowd, roughly 3,000 strong, spread between the mountain, the hillock to its north and lower ground between the two (see Map 5). They look peaceful, not threatening anyone. Yet, additional armed police were rapidly brought to the field around the mountain, and some were manoeuvred into new positions, effectively encircling the workers. Much of this build-up was watched by strikers still sitting on the mountain. The media quickly retreated from just below the mountain to a safer position, from where they would record the opening of the massacre.[43] Mineworker 8 reveals Lonmin's direct involvement. Two 'big joined buses from the mine' arrived delivering yet more police to the scene. Also 'soldiers' appeared on top of their Hippos (these were probably Hippos of the classic kind). We later learned there were vehicles from each of the neighbouring provinces, but it seems there was even one, perhaps more, from the Eastern Cape. Mineworker 4 tells of strikers talking to homeboys from towns in the Transkei, and a witness quoted by Greg Marinovich mentioned that he'd been told that an Eastern Cape policeman had claimed 'there was

First blood.
Photographs
taken just after
TV footage
appeared to
show workers
charging at
the police.

The massacre

a paper signed allowing them to shoot'.[44] Mineworker 8 says: 'What really amazed me was that the truck that carries water and the other one that carries tear gas, they were nowhere near, they were standing right at the back'. Ominously, mine ambulances were already present when the shooting started.[45]

A major concern for the strikers was seeing the police rapidly reel out the razor wire using two or more Hippos. See Map 5. This shows the approximate position of the wire, which was positioned in a line northwards from a pylon close to the electrical power facility and then took a turn to the right in the direction of a small kraal (the first of three in that area). Mineworker 2 said they were being 'closed in with a wire like we were cows', and one of the miners' wives said that the fencing was for 'rats and dogs'.[46] The comments are significant because the police had begun treating the workers as if they were no longer human beings. A group of the miners' leaders, including Mambush, tried to remonstrate with the police near a point marked + on Map 5. Their plea that a gap be left open, so that strikers could leave like human beings, fell on deaf ears. With guns aimed at the workers, it was clear that the police were now ready to shoot. A large number of the strikers rushed north-eastwards in the direction of Nkaneng, where many of them lived.

It was now that the first shot was fired. According to members of our Reference Group, this came from behind the miners who were heading towards Nkaneng, from the north-west, and killed a worker at a point close to the second + on Map 5. Some fleeing strikers, including several leaders, now turned towards the right, hoping to escape through a small gap between the wire and the first kraal. Most continued onwards, so there were no hoards of armed warriors following this leading group, as suggested in some media coverage, though not by TV footage. One woman, a witness, later made the point that the strikers were running with their weapons down, and so were not a threat, and this can be seen in some photographs.[47] It was too late. The leaders' path was blocked by Hippos, and they were trapped. Mineworker 2 recalled: 'People were not killed because they were fighting... We were shot while running. [We] went through the hole, and that is why we were shot.'

The order was given to fire. The command probably came from a white man, who did so, according to Mineworker 6, using the word 'Red'.[48] There were no warning shots.[49] According to Mineworker 2, who was clearly present, 'the first person who started to shoot was a soldier in a Hippo, and he never fired a warning shot, he just shot straight at us'. Within seconds seven workers had been slain, killed by automatic gunfire right in front of TV cameras (see Map 5). In photographs, their bodies are pictured in a pile, with a shack nearby. Moments later, another group of five men were killed, their bodies crushed against a kraal, as if cornered without any possibility of escape. Mineworker 8 questioned: 'I get very amazed when the police say they were defending themselves, what were they defending themselves from?'

Some of the leading group, including Mambush, were able to turn back. They joined other workers scattering in all directions. Many fled north; some went westwards in the hope of reaching Marikana; others just ran as far as they could and as quickly as their legs would carry them; and one, at least, crawled a long distance across ground, hoping to dodge bullets and Hippos.[50] It is difficult to imagine how terrifying and disorienting the situation must have been. There were armoured vehicles all around; there were helicopters in the sky; horses charging to and fro; police sweeping through on foot; stun grenades making a noise as loud as a bomb; tear gas; water cannons; rubber bullets; live rounds; and people being injected with syringes. This was not public order policing, this was warfare. A strike leader remarked: 'Water, which is often used to warn people, was used later on, after a lot of people were shot at already'.[51] Perhaps confirming this, on 20 August we found blue-green water-canon dye in an arc well to the west of the mountain, far from the initial front line. Similarly, Mineworker 10 asserted: 'They lied about rubber bullets. They did not use them.' I have not heard of the use of injections before, and it remains to be seen why they were used and to what effect. There were many complaints that workers were trampled to death by Hippos.[52] Some had been made dizzy by tear gas and some had stumbled perhaps.[53] Some people we spoke to described deceased workers whose bodies were so badly crushed they could only be identified by finger prints. Helicopters used a range of weapons.

Of the 34 workers who were slaughtered on 16 August, 12 died in the opening encounter. About eight died in various locations around the battlefield. The remainder were killed in one small location. This is the place known by the Inquiry as Kleinkopje. But South Africa is littered with small koppies and it seems more appropriate to call it Killing Koppie. Here, some 300 metres to the west of the mountain, on a low rocky outcrop covered with shrubs and trees, the police killed 13 or 14 workers. On a grassy plane with few large bushes this was an obvious place to hide from bullets and Hippos, but it was relatively easy for the police to encircle and then move in for the kill. Two helicopters came from the north, depositing their paramilitary cargo, and two or three Hippos moved in from the south. Mineworker 9 told us: 'That is where some of our members went in and never came back... the people who ran into the bush were ones being transported [in ambulances and police trucks]'. On 20 August, when we were directed to the Killing Koppie, we not only found letters on the rocks that had been spray-painted in yellow, marking sites from where bodies had been removed, we also saw pools and rivulets of dried blood discoloured by the blue-green dye. Mineworker 5 was present on the Koppie; one of those lucky to survive. He recalls: 'You were shot if you put up your hands.' Needless to say, he did not raise his hands. Rather, he says: 'I was taken by a gentleman who was of Indian ancestry. He held me and when I tried to stand up I was hit with guns, and he stopped them.' A drop of humanity in a sea of bestiality. Some workers were disarmed and then speared by the police (we heard this from a number of strikers including Mineworker 5). Whatever view one takes of the initial killings, it is clear that the men who died on the Killing Koppie were fleeing from the battlefield. Moreover, the precise locations of deaths and the autopsy evidence tend to reinforce the account provided by Mineworker 5, leading one to the conclusion that Killing Koppie was the site of cold-blooded murder.[54]

Immediate aftermath

Those who were arrested had to suffer ill-treatment and torture. Soon after his arrest, Mineworker 5 was told by police, spitefully it seems

Yellow letters at Killing Coppie indicating where the bodies of 'G' and 'H' were found.

to me: 'Right here we have made many widows... we have killed all these men.' As with most of the other arrested survivors, he was initially held at a Lonmin facility known as B3. He pondered: 'It seemed as though the police did not belong to the government, but that they belonged to the company.' Later he was taken to a police station, where he had to sleep on a cement floor without a blanket (in the middle of winter), received only bread and tea without sugar, was unable to take his TB medication, and was refused a call to his children even though he was a widower. Other detainees were tortured. Early in the struggle, Mineworker 8 thought the police would protect the workers from NUM. After the massacre he was venomous: 'I will just look at them and they are like dogs to me now... when I see a police now I feel like throwing up... I do not trust them anymore, they are like enemies.'

The massacre was an intensely traumatic experience for all its victims. Mineworker 1 recalled: 'We had pain on the 16th, but it was more painful... on the 17th... because [if] one [comrade] did not come back... we did not know if he had died or what'. Mineworker 8 drew on his knowledge of history, but this did not hide his suffering. 'Hey my man,' he started, 'my head was not working on that day and I was very, very numb and very, very nervous, because I was scared. I never knew of such things. I only knew of them like what had happened in 1976 and what happened in 1992, because of history.' Linking this back to the present, he continued: 'I would hear about massacres you see. I usually heard of that from history, but on that day it came back, so that I can see it. Even now, when I think back, I feel terrible, and when I reverse my thinking to that, I feel sad, still.'[55] For Mineworker 10, trauma was linked with a political assessment. He started: 'I am still traumatised by the incident. Even when I see it on TV, I still get scared because I could not sleep the days following the incident.' He then concluded: 'It is worse because this has been done to us by a government we thought, with Zuma in power, things would change. But we are still oppressed and abused.'

The bloodshed, cruelty and sorrow of the massacre could have led to the collapse of the strike. That is what Lonmin, the police and NUM had expected. But it was not to be. Somehow, surviving leaders managed to rally the workers and stiffen their resolve to win the fight. This must have taken great courage and determination. Eventually, the company did agree to talk to the workers. Having done so, it conceded large increases in pay (22 per cent for RDOs) plus a R2,000 return-to-work bonus.[56] When this was announced on 18 September, it was greeted by the workers as a victory, as indeed it was. The scale of this achievement was soon reflected in a massive wave of unprotected strikes, led by rank-and-file committees, which spread from platinum mining, into gold, and on to other minerals, with ripples extending further into other South African industries. 34 workers were murdered by the police on the battlefield at Marikana, but they did not die in vain.

Notes

1 Where I have referred to a particular mineworker as the source of information (e.g. Mineworker 8), the reader can read the related interview later in the book.
2 Peter Alexander, 'Oscillating Migrants, "Detribalised Families" and Militancy: Mozambicans on Witbank Collieries, 1918–1927,' *Journal of Southern African Studies* 27(3) (2001), p. 522.
3 The housing allowance was not paid to workers staying in hostels (where,

according to Mineworker 9, a room is shared by eight residents). There is controversy about the pay received by RDOs and other workers, and this is considered in a note below.

4   See Malcolm Rees, 'Credit Regulator swoops on Marikana micro-lenders', *MoneyWeb*, 9 October 2012.

5   We heard complaints that bribery was sometimes necessary to gain employment and might assist with obtaining an NUM bursary. For women, sex could be used as payment. This was alluded to by Mineworker 7. See also Mineworker 8, and Asanda P. Benya, 'Women in Mining: A Challenge to Occupational Culture in Mines', MA dissertation, University of the Witwatersrand, 2009, specifically pp. 84–86.

6   Reuters Africa, 'Lonmin starts sacking 9,000 Marikana strikers', *Reuters Africa*, 24 May 2011. The NUM says: 'We emphatically deny that we advised Lonmin to dismiss 9,000 striking employees' (letter from Frans Baleni to Peter Alexander, 5 December 2012). However, given the union's lack of support for the workers' action, one can forgive workers who assumed that the NUM had not contested the sackings strongly enough..

7   Mineworker 8. Although listed on the London Stock Exchange, Lonmin's operational headquarters are in Johannesburg. All its production takes place in South Africa, and a very high proportion of this occurs in Marikana, where, in addition to the three mines, there is a Process Division that includes concentrators, a smelter and a base metal refinery. Each mine has several shafts. In 2011, Lonmin had a total of 27,796 employees. Lonmin Plc, *Building for the Future* (Lonmin Plc, London, 2011), pp 1–2.

8   See interview with Joseph Mathunjwa. This is to be found later in the book.

9   See speech by Jeff Mphahlele. This is to be found later in the book.

10 In addition to our interviews, this narrative draws on contributions made by members of a reference group (hereafter Reference Group), which assembled at the University of Johannesburg on 15 October. The group included 16 workers, some of whom led the strike, plus six wives and girlfriends. Joseph Mathunjwa and Jimmy Gama, AMCU's treasurer, also participated. We are greatly indebted to all the participants.

11 Reference Group.

12 Mineworker 1.

13 Reference Group. See also *SA Labour News*, 14 August 2012.

14 See speeches later in the book.

15 If the intention was to secure a cost-to-company package of R12,500, the gap between what RDOs were being paid and what they wanted was relatively moderate. According to Lonmin, the average RDOs cost-to-company package was R9,812.98. It broke this down as follows. Basic cash component: R5,404; pension contribution: R801; medical aid allowance: R556; housing allowance: R1,850; holiday leave allowance: R450; RDOs allowance: R750. Of these elements, the pension contribution and medical aid and holiday leave allowances were excluded from the monthly pay transfer, and the RDO allowance had only just been won, so it was not included either. This leaves the basic cash component

and the housing allowance, which totalled R7,250. Once we allow for tax and other deductions, the gap between what the employers said they paid and what the workers said they received was modest, though further research is required to explain the remaining difference. If workers did not work a full month or had garnishee orders, this would reduce their 'take home' pay. Monica Laganparsad, 'Just how much does a miner make?' *Business Live*, 26 August 2012. Downloaded from www.timeslive.co.za on 19 November 2012. Garnishee orders require employers to deduct money from a worker's salary to settle a debt of some kind. They are common in South Africa, especially in the mining industry.

16　Mineworker 1.

17　Mineworker 6.

18　Lonmin reported that in 2011 women were 4.3 per cent of its employees in 'core mining operations'. Lonmin, *Building for the Future*, p. 77.

19　Mineworkers 1 and 2.

20　Mineworkers 1 and 8.

21　Speech by Bhele, see later in the book.

22　Mineworker 8.

23　See speech later in the book.

24　As if signalling its allegiance, NUM shares a house with the Congress of South African Trade Unions (COSATU), the South African Communist Party (SACP), and the governing party, the African National Congress (ANC). The neighbouring house is a small police station.

25　While the workers were firm in their recollections, the body has never been found.

26　Jared Sacks, 'Marikana prequel: NUM and the murders that started it all', *The Maverick*, 18 October 2012.

27　Mineworker 4.

28　The full statement from Tip reads: 'It is believed that the marchers had malicious intent and upon their arrival in the vicinity of the NUM offices a confrontation ensued between the marchers and a number of NUM members during which firearms were discharged. Although there already appeared to be differing versions regarding this incident, NUM will in due course lead evidence that in the circumstances the use of firearms by NUM members was justified.

29　Mineworker 1. This use of the term *boer* (literally 'farmer' in Afrikaans) implies whites linked with forces of repression, such as the police and army. In practice, dating back to apartheid, most are Afrikaans-speaking, but they could be English-speaking, and not all Afrikaans-speakers are regarded as *boere*. Our interviewees tend to use the term 'Hippo' to refer to all armoured vehicles. Technically this is incorrect. The Hippo, developed for use in South Africa's border war and used against township protests, was replaced by the Casspir in 1978/9. Another frequently deployed armoured personnel carrier is the Nyala, which was specifically designed for riot control, Hippos/Casspirs are larger and with a higher wheel base than the Nyala.

30　According to Greg Marinovich, 'The Cold Murder Fields of Marikana', *Daily Maverick*, 8 September 2012, the miners were killed by helicopter gunfire. Ten people died in conflicts before 16 August. Our account refers to eight of these, but none of our informants could assist us with details about the other two.

31　Reference Group participant.

32　Fanakalo is a lingua franca developed on the mines during the twentieth century to facilitate communication between workers coming from many different language backgrounds, and between them and their bosses. It is based on Nguni languages, which include isiZulu and isiXhosa (the home language of most Marikana miners), with occasional words from other African languages, including Setswana (the main local tongue), and English and Afrikaans. Fanakalo is frowned upon by some of the more politicised workers, who see it as an oppressors' language, and the mining companies now use English as an official language, but Fanakalo is still widely spoken.

33　Mineworker 3.

34　Mineworker 3.

35　See speech later in the book.

36　Mineworker 8.

37　Mineworker 8.

38　Mineworker 8.

39　Mineworkers 8 and 9.

40　Mineworker 10.

41　Speech by Jeff Mphahlele.

42　Mineworker 2.

43　Mineworker 6.

44　Marinovich, 'The Cold Murder Fields of Marikana'.

45　Mineworker 8.

46　Interview with wife of a mineworker.

47　Genevieve Quintal, 'Marikana commission, observers visit hostels, site of shootings', *Business Day*, 3 October 2012.

48　See also speech by Bhele later in the book.

49　See speech by a strike leader later in the book.

50　Mineworker 4.

51　See speech later in the book.

52　Mineworkers 1, 2 and 8.

53　Mineworker 10.

54　See Marinovich, 'The Cold Murder Fields of Marikana'.

55　'1976' is a reference to the Soweto Uprising. '1992' refers to the Boipatong Massacre and/or the Bisho Massacre. This interview was conducted on 19 September, more than a month after the massacre.

56　Increases ranged from 11 to 22 per cent. RDOs pay was hiked from about R9080 per month to R11,078 per month (the former being a lower figure than the one previously provided by the employer) (see note above).

3

Background interviews

Undertaken by Thapelo Lekgowa and Peter Alexander

Joseph Mathunjwa, President, Association of Mineworkers and Construction Union

JOSEPH MUTHUNJWA: I was born in 1965. I am from the family of priesthood under the Salvation Army. The relatives of my mother were located around Johannesburg, Witbank, Ermelo. Some were mineworkers. After my high school I came to Witbank looking for a job. I couldn't go to further education, my father was not getting paid enough to assist. I started working in construction around Witbank, close to the mines. Then I went to Tweefontein Colliery. I was not long there. Then I went to Douglas Colliery. I was working in a laboratory and later in the materials department, but these were not regarded as white-collar jobs, because within the very same departments those jobs were also classified for coloureds, Indians and whites. We were under categories 3 to 8 in those days, but they were on higher categories.

INTERVIEWER: Do you remember the 1987 strike? As I recall one of the issues in Witbank was about workers wanting to make the hostels family hostels.

JM: I remember that one. It lasted for a month. I think it was a combination of many things, not really hostels per se. It was called by NUM.

INTERVIEWER: From then, through to when AMCU was formed, it was 13 years or something like that, do you have strong memories of work in that period?

JM: I think from '86 my presence at work was felt because I didn't wait to join a union to express how I see things. Firstly, when I realised that we were confined in the hostel, [with] no transport for black workers to take them to the locations [townships], to stay with their families, I was the first black person who jumped into a white [only] bus in 1986, forcing my way to the location. Subsequent to that I was the first black person to enter into a white recreation club within the mine. That led me to many troubles with mine management. I was the first person at Douglas who led a campaign [for] workers to have houses outside the mine premises. So I led many campaigns. That was '86, '86. NUM was there, but it was not really, what can I say, more instrumental about living outside the mine. It was more focused on disciplinary hearing[s], but not this global approach on social issues.

INTERVIEWER: How did you organise?

JM: I would go to the meetings, and people would hear about myself. Then I would go to the general managers' office. All things started when I boarded the white transport by force. Then the managers had very much interest. 'Who is this guy?' They said: 'There's the union'. I said, the union does not address these issues. Then they asked: 'What other issues?' Then I made a list of those issues, and I started a campaign for those issues.

INTERVIEWER: Are there things you remember during the 1990s?

JM: I still remember, there was a Comrade Mbotho, from Pandoland, who passed on, from Pondoland. He was very strong. He was like a chairman of NUM at Van Dyk's Drift. He was a very strong Mpondo man. I remember he organised a big boycott of using those horse-trailer buses, for transporting you from hostel to shaft. How can I explain this? You have the head of the truck which has a link and it pulls like a bus, but semi bus. You cannot see where you are going, you are just inside, like you are transporting horses, race horses. He [the manager] changed the buses to give proper buses to the workers.

INTERVIEWER: Later on you were expelled from NUM, so at some stage you must have joined?

JM: Yes. The workers were aware that there is this young man working in the mine and they said: 'You have to be part of NUM in order [to fight for] all the issues that are affecting workers.' Then I joined NUM, and the management didn't like the manner in which things were raised, and I was transferred... When they saw that I was attending most of the meetings [and] becoming more influential to the workers, they sent me to one of the stores. It's called Redundant Store, where all items that are no longer in use will be parked there. It was like a Robben Island of some sort. You cannot be among the workers; you cannot attend meetings. To attend meetings I had to travel more than 20 kilometres, [and] when you get there the meeting is finished. But nevertheless being part of the NUM, I was elected as a shaft steward. Then I represented workers. I still remember when there was a fatal underground [accident], and the worker died in a very mysterious way, then we were called in. That was my first experience. They [the attorney for the company] wanted us to sign some documents, a prepared document. I said: 'Why should we sign this document?' They said: 'No, it's about the person [who] passed on [so that] we all cover ourselves.' I said: 'Why should we cover ourselves as shaft stewards, when we are not working in that area?' So I defied. Most of the shaft stewards signed those documents.

INTERVIEWER: Were you a shaft steward just for your department, or on the mine itself? How were you organised as an NUM branch?

JM: For the department, on the surface. You've got your branch executive and your shaft steward council. One branch covers one colliery.

INTERVIEWER: And then workers would take their grievance to this shaft steward?

JM: Yes, to the shaft steward. And then shaft steward to the council, because we do have our 'during-the-week meetings', [collecting] all the grievances from different department[s]. Then we go to the mass meeting. We tell them what's happening; then we formulate an agenda to meet with management.

INTERVIEWER: And these days is there complete separation between AMCU and NUM on each of the mines, or are there places where they come together, as shaft stewards perhaps?

Joseph Mathunjwa addresses a rally in Marikana on 20 August 2012.

JM: We are completely separate. NUM will have their shaft steward council and AMCU will have its own. And the only [place] where we meet together, it's where we are dealing with issues like health and safety, employment equity and all those forums, because those are the legislated forums, which don't define a union. But where we are the majority, so AMCU will run the show; in as much [as] NUM is the majority, then they will run the show.

INTERVIEWER: Let's go back to your NUM days.

JM: I became part of the big picture of NUM as a shaft steward. I started raising issues, like bonuses that underground workers were not receiving. Then I started going to management, and said a person who is working underground is not receiving bonuses, while you find a person who is working on the surface is receiving a bonus. How can that work? I managed to fight for that until such time the management paid, which was a big victory. I used to go underground and check how things are working. During that time, foreign workers, especially the Mozambicans, were buried around the mine when they died, so I fought for those workers to be transported back to their place of origin, to be buried by their families. We got the management to provide a 65-seater bus to take people to the funeral. This was a highlight.

INTERVIEWER: Were you on the branch executive?

JM: Later, I became chairman of the branch. After all these things the workers were not happy [and] they [passed] a vote of no confidence in the entire branch executive. Then I was elected with a new committee. So that's when all the things started. Management, in collaboration with NUM, tried to sabotage me, putting some cases against me, and subsequent to that I was sort of dismissed. Then the workers said: 'No, we have to do something, because Joseph was fighting for our cause. So an injury to one, will be an injury to all!' So, they reported for work and, subsequent to that, they never came out from underground.

INTERVIEWER: How long did they stay underground? According to an article I read it was ten days.

JM: Yes, ten days. It was difficult. Sometimes there was no food, no water. They had to drink the water from the roof. They sacrificed. It was the first [underground strike] in the history of mine workers [in South Africa]!

INTERVIEWER: According to this article management reinstated you, and then NUM came along and they said that you were bringing the union into disrepute.

JM: Exactly. I was summoned to be at their head office [for a disciplinary hearing] under the chairmanship of Gwede Mantashe [then general secretary of NUM], which I refused. I mean, Gwede was highly involved. He used to come at the mine and try to split the workers when I was not around—only to find that the workers in the hostel were very united. I still remember, we had a report saying he was chased out... because he came and said wrong things about myself.

INTERVIEWER: So this is all happening in 1999?

JM: Yes.

INTERVIEWER: What about your job?

JM: NUM wrote a letter to management saying that they must terminate [me]. Then management called me, and I said: 'I am not employed by NUM, and as long as my job is secured I will continue working.' [So I stayed] at Van Dyk's Drift.

INTERVIEWER: But you couldn't be in the union?

JM: No, I couldn't be in the union. Subsequent to my expulsion, whatever they call it, the workers called a meeting. They said they are going to resign from NUM, which, of course, they did. They called a meeting, and I was called in. They said I must go and look for a union, which they might join, which I did. I called different unions for interviews. The workers were not happy. So they mandated me to form a union. It's not that I formed a union, I was mandated.

INTERVIEWER: So that's why you formed AMCU. When was the union registered?

JM: In 2001. There was only one branch, at Douglas [i.e. Van Dyk's Drift].

INTERVIEWER: How did you grow? What is the history of the union?

JM: We tried to open a small office in town [Witbank]. I was by myself at that time. There was no secretary. I was doing everything—recruiting, going to CCMA [Commission for Conciliation, Mediation and Arbitration], holding mass meetings—for quite some time.

INTERVIEWER: One of the criticisms is that you were supported by management when you started the union. How do you respond to that?

JM: Those allegations are baseless. There is no management that supported us. It was not a cosy relationship. If you can count how many marches did we throw to them?!... But we maintained our cool. There was no unprotected strike that we ever conducted in Douglas.

INTERVIEWER: So, in those early days, you were concerned to recruit in the collieries?

JM: Yes, but remember our union was more of construction than mineworkers. Construction was also vulnerable, they had no representation whatsoever, so they also came in.

INTERVIEWER: What were the high points and low points between the formation of the union and let's say 2011?

JM: I think the low point was that we were a new union, which everyone was hesitant to join. We did not have any history, and you are only from a single mine, so how can you influence all the mines? That was a challenge. Also, subsequent to our registration, there was a big retrenchment. In 2005, if I'm not mistaken, most of our members were kind of being retrenched. As AMCU, we felt it was a strategy to destabilise the union. NUM signed a three-year retrenchment agreement. We didn't sign. We said we will not sign a three-year agreement, which was just giving workers on a silver platter to the employer. And then our members were retrenched.

INTERVIEWER: Which colliery was that at?

JM: It was across BHP Billiton mines [which included Van Dyk's Drift]. We took that matter to the Labour Court. That was our highlight. It took time and was strenuous, but we got a ruling in our favour. The court ruled in favour of AMCU, that the company was un-procedural—substantively unfair—to dismiss our members. So they had to reinstate them. I think from there, through word of mouth [about] how AMCU played itself, being a small union in the big environment turned to be very positive.

INTERVIEWER: How did you get members in other provinces?

JM: It was word of mouth. Families go back home—'There is this union, guys, you must try this union'. Also, our achievement in terms of winning cases; respecting the mandate from the workers; not taking decision without having a mandate; constantly calling mass meetings; engaging workers.

INTERVIEWER: Which were the provinces where you grew?

JM: Mpumalanga, and then we had KZN also growing.

INTERVIEWER: When did workers in platinum start joining AMCU.

JM: I would say 2010. Later, there was a dismissal at Lonmin. Some were re-employed and some were not. So they approached us. We had members who were shaft sinkers at Lonmin, on a contract. So, based on that, when people asked around, they said 'Why don't you go and try this union'.

INTERVIEWER: What happened at Impala? The strike this year?

JM: Yes, the Impala strike, early 2012. The managers chased us away there, even before the strike. After the strike, people phoned us. They said: 'We want to join your union'.

INTERVIEWER: So nobody can say that this strike was called by AMCU?

JM: It is wrong to suggest that. After the strike we went there, and they wanted the forms. They filled them out and gave them to us. They were tired of NUM.

INTERVIEWER: One of the other things I've heard said, probably by someone from NUM, is that 'AMCU is just a one man show'. How do you respond to that idea?

JM: What do they mean by that? Oh, okay. If it's me, then it means there would be no conferences; there would no elections; no regional structures; no shaft steward council. It's baseless. It's the last kick of a dying horse.

INTERVIEWER: Why did you affiliate to NACTU?

JM: When AMCU was registered we requested to be affiliated to COSATU. That was our first stop. They referred us to NUM. They said they've got a union that represents mining, so we need to join hands with NUM. I said, 'But you guys know very well what happened,' so we went to NACTU.

INTERVIEWER: What's your view about having women working on the mines?

JM: I mean it's not really a very conducive place for women, especially underground—heavy machines—it's not. But we cannot say they must not work, because it's more exposure and diversity and so forth.

INTERVIEWER: Do you have any women who are shaft stewards for AMCU?

JM: Yes, we do. They even serve in the regional structures.

INTERVIEWER: Do they raise issues which are special for women, like being harassed underground?

JM: They do participate in terms of amenities. Women are not catered for.

INTERVIEWER: Are you opposed to migrant labour, would you like it to be stopped?

JM: Before, we had no borders in Africa. So it was colonisation who came with borders.

INTERVIEWER: How do people communicate in a meeting if they are coming with different languages?

JM: They use Fanakalo. It's quite a lot of Zulu and Shangaan. It's not really a good language, but it's been there for years, so it's a means of communication, to pass the message across.

INTERVIEWER: Do you think some miners joined AMCU because it accepts Fanakalo, whereas NUM is more critical?

JM: No. When workers join AMCU they feel a sigh of relief. AMCU, one should understand, is an apolitical union. So it's a union that still works with the mandate and the politics of the workplace. So our decisions are not contaminated by any external influence of politics. They are determined by the members, and our job as leaders is just to guide and advise them.

A rock drill operator at work.

A rock drill operator

ROCK DRILL OPERATOR: I wake up at 3:30am and have to be out of the house by 4am. I walk a distance of about 1.2 kilometres [and] that is where I catch the 4:15 bus. This bus only drops me off at K3 shaft, so I have to take another bus again that will drop me off at the hostel. Then I take the third bus that drops me here at 4B. The first thing I have to do when I get to work is check in properly. There are no dispatch[es] [lift] so we all have to take a chair lift from surface to level 1, then another from level 2 to 6 [and] take another chair lift from level 6 to 10. That is where I work. When I arrive I still have to walk another distance of 800 metres to the waiting place. That is where I change my white overall [or jump suit] and wear old clothes because the machine[s] we use are very greasy and might badly stain the white overall.

The team leader has to make sure that there is enough air for breathing. I also have to make sure that there is enough wires for water and pipes. It is not easy operating a machine. The size of the drilling stick [drill bit] is very long [and] sometimes we use 2.4-metre-long which is the most preferred or alternatively use the 1.8-metre-long stick [drill bit]. There are two of us who operate these machines and we each have our own machines. We first have to provide support. After that we use the 3-metre-long stick. That is what we use to check for water [and] we use it to drill 3 holes, then we use the 2.4-metres to drill more holes. In a day, we usually drill about 40 holes.

The job of being an RDO requires a lot of discipline so if you drink and like woman at the same time you have to choose one and sacrifice the other because this job requires a lot of dedication and hard work. Another thing is that the working conditions here in the mine are not that good at all. There are strict rules as to what you can and cannot do, but even if you follow their rules you will still get into trouble for not blasting or doing this and that. It's confusing because they advise us not to take chances but when you follow the rules they still question you, so this is one of the challenges we face as RDO[s]. Secondly, the PPE [Personal Protective Equipment] we use to work is not 100 per cent safe because, for example, if you use a pair of gloves today to operate the machine you cannot use the same pair tomorrow because it will be full of grease and they order us to use the same gloves over and over again. How are you going to use the same gloves that have grease? Even the overalls they give us a new pair once in every six months, they then complain when we bring our own clothes from home to wear them when we drill the machine, so you never know what these people want. At the end of the shift we have to pack the machines and do what we call charging holes [putting explosives in the holes].

All these jobs are done by us RDOs [since] we lack mining assistants here [in Karee]. As I mentioned before, that is the job I used to do before I came here so here in this mine they lack such people who are responsible for that job, so now we have to do extra jobs. After all that we have to go and take [a] bath. We prefer sunlight liquid because it removes the grease easily compared to [a] solid bar. There is also the issue of water. Sometimes there is not even water [the showers are not enough to handle the capacity of men] so we [are] forced to go home looking all greasy and dirty because... there are few lockers [in the changing rooms] so we do not have space to store our clothes. So I am forced to wear the same thing from home to work and back home again because I do not have a place where I can change my clothes. So I have to wash the clothes myself at home.

Another challenge is that in the morning the chairlifts work but in the afternoon they do not work and we have to walk all the way up. That is affecting us a lot. Sometimes the bus even delay[s] us and this whole thing that a person works [a] standard eight hours a day... does not apply to us here in the mine. Here we work ten to twelve hours a day. All the management cares about is that we blast and bore the machine and blast. Whether you work extra hours or not, they do not care about that. We are the first to arrive here at work and the last to leave. [This is] unlike wheel [winch] operators who stick to normal working hours—they find us here and leave us here. That is why we as drill operators were complaining because we do the hardest job. To give you an example, women who work here in the mines they also do other jobs like engineering... and in the other mines they work as winch operators and loco drivers but you will never find even one woman who work[s] as [an] RDO.

In the olden days people who worked as RDO[s] were considered to be uneducated. That is why they used to group RDOs and winch operator[s] together. At the time, winch operators were considered to be more smart and they performed the easy tasks but got paid more than RDOs. But now things have changed [and] we realise it is not fair that we do the hardest work but still get paid peanuts. If RDOs, were to decide not to work for a day, the whole mine will be on a standstill because there is no job without us. Even though we got more money after the strike, we still feel it is not enough because RDOs perform the hardest job especially here at Karee. [This is] because one person is responsible for operating one machine by themselves without any assistance, as compared to Western where people work in pairs, here you work by yourself without any assistant. And if you look at it, if anything had to go wrong, for instance the air-pipes were to break, then the assistant will be the one who will immediately assist you. But now we suffer because you have to do everything by yourself. And when you operate the machine it has to function in the same direction [There are markings on rocks done by engineers indicating the exact position one must drill]. You do not just go in your own direction. It must be kept in the line that has been painted red.

Operating the machine is the most difficult task and you cannot go home until you have completed your daily task. The stress sometimes causes us to make accidents. Because you are constrained by time you always have to watch the time [and] make sure you finish in time. When I knock off work the first thing I do is to take a bath and after that I eat and sleep. If you notice as a rock driller if you go on the 35 days leave it feels like six months and you gain a bit of weight. Even if you miss two days of work the third day your whole body becomes sore when you go back to work because you are used to working all the time—it is like a gym to us [if you skip a few days of gym upon return your body reacts with pain]. I am not going to lie to you, this is the most difficult job any one can ever do and most people do not want to do this job because it does not only require physical strength but also [a] sharp mind, so it is a combination of both mental and physical alertness that is required to perform this job. That is why I say this job requires two people not one. So [this] job is not an easy one.

… Those people who were saying that RDOs are machine boys who are illiterate what do they need R12,500 for? They are still using the old school excuse [and this is because] they have no idea how difficult the job of an RDO is at all. [That is why they think] that we deserved peanuts. Even the superiors who come to observe us when we work they never stay for more than thirty minutes because they can see for themselves how difficult the job is. Even the raincoats [wet suits] we use you will not want to see it the following day because it is very dirty, but we have no choice but to reuse it so that we can avoid being sick and prevent ourselves from being wet, which may alternatively result in being sick.

The wife of a mineworker

INTERVIEWER: All the women that came out [to the rally on 18 September] are you here to support your husbands?

Marikana: A View from the Mountain and a Case to Answer

Women from around Marikana make their views known, 18 August 2012.

WIFE OF MINEWORKER: Yes. I am here to support my husband. He has 27 years working here. He earns R3,000 [per month]. He starts work in the morning at 3am and knocks off at 2:30pm... Which policeman can say he's living a good life earning R3,000 for 27 years? This is the 27th year since he's here, now the police are carrying wire. They are fencing for rats and dogs there in the mountain, they are killing them. They [workers] are crying, crying for their money and... SABC 1 is lying. There is nothing like 'it's the miner that started attacking the police', it's the police that started. We all stood in the neighbourhood crying tears, they were not even doing anything there. Our husbands are lost, we haven't seen them up to today. Here we are being evicted by the landlords, they want their money for rent and there is not money for rent. Our husbands were not paid and for me to say [that] my husband has 27 years here, 27 years but he earns a cent and he's going to be killed for that cent... Now we want those men that were locked up, wherever they are locked up [to come back home].

INTERVIEWER: Were there people arrested?

WIFE OF MINEWORKER: Yes... The Hippo is not for running over people [like it did on the day of the massacre]. [The] Hippo is for fighting crime. Our husbands are prisoners there, they are dead... We want our husbands... When I cry my husband is here close by. We want our husbands. We want to sleep with our husbands, do you hear me? They, the police, sleep with their wives, we want our husband to come and sleep with us.

The other thing I want to say, police are failing to catch thieves. These people [who were shot and arrested] are working here. They are just marching, then the police are arresting them, they were not arrested near the mine. It's not in the mine on the road where people were arrested. In those houses, they just saw police beating them up and arresting and shooting at them when they did nothing wrong. Has anyone ever worked to earn 4,000? You that is working and getting 100,000 because of that person [who is doing the hard work underground], why don't you give him the amount that he wants? [Instead] you have to wait until they fight.

No one is to be shot. It's not apartheid now. The police have no right to shoot at something... and let it [the vehicle] run over someone, pour poison over someone and shoot them. When he tries to run away, they run over him. They were not shot in the mine area... And my brother, they are wrong when they arrived there, they told their relatives to remain behind. The miners had their *intonga* [traditional walking stick] and they wanted to talk but the police came with guns and said: 'Why are they carrying sticks?' Now we don't want 5,000, we want 15,000 now.

4

Speeches

Speech given by Tholakele 'Bhele' Dlunga (a strike leader) to a rally on a field by Nkaneng, on 18 August 2012

Amandla [the power]! Awethu [is ours]! Viva workers, viva! Eish these airplanes [circling above the crowd of about 15,000 workers who were sitting very quietly and still on the grass outside Nkaneng] are disturbing us—let us continue regardless. Okay, okay every one please be silent, I am going to use my language to address you, but I will try and make sure that we all understand each other. As workers we are all gathered in this place. For those who do not know this started on the 9th when workers of Lonmin gathered to try and address the issue of wage dissatisfaction, we all gathered on the 9th to try [and] get our heads together and find a way forward. We want to get decent wages so that we can be able to support our families. We call ourselves workers but we are still suffering. We met on the 9th and took a decision that on the 10th [we] will take a short walk to Number 1, to our employer. On our way there the owner sent his white securities to stop us before we reached the offices. They told us that they were aware of our plan. We were shocked because we did not tell him what our demands were, yet how did he find out?

They said we should wait for the employer and his team. They were still in a meeting. 15 minutes passed then 30 minutes still waiting for him. We decided to go near the office. The security guards came back again, but this time around they were accompanied by police who built a wall around the premises... We told the police that, 'we only came here to address our employer, we have no issue with you. The one who employed us to work at Lonmin is there and we will explain to him why we came here when we address him directly.' Three hours passed while we still begged him to give us answers. The situation intensified and we saw that the police wanted to shoot at us. We took a united decision that we will not leave without a direct answer from our employer. A word came that our claims should not [have] been taken into consideration because we went behind our lawyer's back to come and address our employer ourselves.

... [we left and later] we plotted our next plan of action since we failed the first time. On Friday together with other members we went to... the people that were on night duty that day [and then we] decided not [to] pitch for work until our cries were heard. We parted on the agreement that we will meet again on Saturday at the same place at 7am. We then decided since we have lost the first round, to go and meet with our lawyers to tell them [what had happened]. We admitted that we took a wrong turn, but we needed a solution. But on our way there [to the NUM offices on 11 August] we were shot at [by NUM] upon which we lost two of our members. That is where we decided that death waits for no one and we run for our lives and hide in the mountain fearing for our lives. The police preyed on our vulnerability and arrested those they could get their hands on.

The day before yesterday [Thursday 16 August]... they brought a barbed wire [fence] and closed the road on us so we couldn't cross. We don't want to be prevented from expressing ourselves, we didn't steal anything from anyone, we were only demonstrating for one reason only [that is] to have decent wages and what they did is they responded by firing guns at us. Some were luckier than others, they managed to dodge the bullets, indeed hospitals are full with Lonmin workers. The police were working with soldiers [and] they even said that we must be destroyed but we didn't wrong any one, we were only fighting for our rights. Why must we die? All we were doing is fight[ing] for our rights and we did not kill anyone. Why must we then be killed? Now I am going to hand over to someone else.

Speech given by a strike leader to a rally on a field by Nkaneng, on 18 August 2012

Amandla! Awethu! I humbly stand in front of you today. Everything that happened that day [16 August] I witnessed it first hand. I also took refuge at that mountain top. My people, when I was at that

A small section of the rally on 18 August 2012.

mountain I was shot at by four police behind me. I was approached by four soldiers riding on horses. I tried calling on to my fellow brothers not to go to Marikana and come this side, but my brothers run towards the police. What happened was that my colleague is now lying at Wonderkop hospital fighting for his life... Another young man who was also my colleague was wearing [a] white T-shirt and blue trousers was also in [the] *Daily Sun* newspapers. Workers we started negotiating with the police on Tuesday afternoon [14 August] at 5pm. They said, 'Workers we are trying to be friendly with you, we are not fighting.' They then requested us to put our weapons down. Five of us then approached the police. Out of the five only three of us were left, but I don't even know where the other two people are today.

On our way there I was asked to ride at the back of a police van. Inside the van I found a white man. He approached me in his language, but as a black person I was expected to speak in his language. This is the same white man who said they wanted to build friendly relations with me. I said if that is the case, let us step outside and go and talk. He replied and said he has the right, which was granted to him by the government so he can only address me privately. I turned around and told the workers that the white man refused to come and address them directly. He said, 'The government gave us the job and the workers' union.' I said, 'Thank you.' and went back to the workers and we all sat down, we all met and talked.

After performing our daily duties we went back to the mines. Our mothers and sisters didn't know where we were staying. We stayed at the mountain top. The police came back... They sent a black person accompanied by a white man and woman to come and address us. They said they came in peace. The police pointed guns at us. We went and spoke to them. I asked him [the police officer] to give me his name. He said to me he cannot do that, he was sent here by his employee. They gave me his name and said it was William Mpembe...

I made it clear to them that we wanted their employer, but they said they were sent by the government. I tried, my fellow workers, until the sun set, but I told them I won't talk to them, I will only talk to their employer. Zokwana [the NUM president] came [and] when I looked at the time it was 6 o'clock, it was already sunset. When Zokwana came with his Hippo the white man came again saying that once again he was asking for friendship. My fellow workers, while I was still addressing the people, Zokwana arrived. I told him that he, 'must come down on this Hippo he is riding and address the workers with respect.'... He said he, 'didn't come here to address us.' He told us that he is requesting us to go back to the mine. I said, 'Is that your final word?' And he said, 'Yes I am done.' He took the speaker from me and said he was addressing the workers. My fellow workers I came back to the people and asked for a phone with a camera. I was given a phone with a camera at the Hippo. The white man came and said, 'Don't shoot me' and every one took for cover.

I was fortunate the police [who] came was the only one with a uniform with words 'P Motswana'. The rest of the police were wearing private clothes with bullet-proof vests... I came back on Thursday together with a young man called Mambush and an old man called Bete who is not here with us at the moment. We said to them, 'Arrest us so that I can go and find the man who signed our death warrant, where our owner and the union took a decision to remove us from the mountain.' My fellow workers now here is the place our president of the AMCU has arrived. He gave us the explanation he got from the employers of Lonmin and it said that it 'doesn't have employees that live in a mountain. All the workers that took refuge in the mountain should be killed, they don't have workers that live in the mountain.'

I was amazed when some members of the AMCU left and they started a song that said, 'What did we do?' This is really painful. We have suffered long enough... When they passed the mountain next to the shacks in the area, the white man said, 'Come'. Lonmin issued six Quantums [a minibus made by Toyota]. While still watching that, a bus from Midbank [bus company] arrived delivering police this side accompanied by the six Quantums also delivering police. I shouted from the mountain and said, 'Zizi your time has come.' When the police stood up to leave they said, 'Lion is leaving now.' When we looked down we saw a car carrying soldiers. They said the Hippo carrying soldiers must come in. When it came in the workers were already on their way out. The white man pointed at all the Hippos and started firing bullets at the people. It didn't shoot at the open space, it shot at the people. Some of the bullets came from the helicopter. That is where I was shot at by four policemen from the airplane. One bullet hit a young man next to me who was wearing a yellow T-shirt who immediately fell to the ground. Bullets started flying all over the place, workers ran for their lives. My fellow workers I ran for my life. I was targeted by a helicopter. When I ran away, there was a young man who is unfortunately not with us today who said, 'If you don't want to die take off your jersey and wear mine instead.' I threw my jersey away and took his jersey. I don't even know how I got here. I ran for my life while bullets were being shot at me.

Water which is often used to warn people was used later on after a lot of people were shot at already. Soldiers concentrated all their efforts on people, people took cover at the nearest bush and by then they were using tear gases accompanied with water all thrown at people. These are all the things I witnessed. I ran to a shack and asked my brother Dlangamandla to give my mother a letter. I was fetched by my mother from this shack and I told them I wanted to know from the councillor whether or not he/she has any knowledge of all this that is being done by the police. My fellow workers arrived at the councillor['s] office accompanied by some woman, but the helicopter was still on my trail. The councillor told me that the only thing he had knowledge of is that workers went and joined the NUM, the same NUM that shot at them without hearing the complaints of the people first. While still on that I explained the whole situation to him and he said he will call the commissioner from Marikana and will request him to go to the mountain where all this conflict took place. My fellow workers I tried my best, the councillor used my phone to call the commissioner who said he only ordered the police to handle the situation, but he was unavailable at the moment where all the conflict was taking place. I think I said everything I needed to say.

Speech given by Jeff Mphahlele (general secretary of AMCU) to a public meeting at the University of Johannesburg, on 20 August 2012

Comrades, I should be grateful that I am alive today. I was involved, I saw what happened… This began four weeks back when Lonmin management invited our president to a meeting requesting assistance. Because there were these rock drillers who were going to come and present a memorandum, and our president Joseph Mathunjwa spontaneously said that they should not entertain that. [He said that]… they should be inviting all relevant structures referring to the big unions [and] the small…

We got a message loud and clear that the employees of Lonmin were demanding 12,500. And it is sad when, what is happening now, when the company it's so stupid. It's able to come out on television and say we have lost R700 million in two days … and I think it is highly unfair for a company to put its profits before the lives of individuals, and that is what exactly happened. And immediately then I got the message loud and clear that 'No, we are not here because of NUM and not because of AMCU, and we have taken this decision to be here on our own as employees of Lonmin'. And comrades, maybe you also need to understand that as AMCU we only command a majority on the other side, which is Karee… So then we took the message to management and… [they] confirmed that 'yes, indeed we have received the demand of R12,500, and "yes" our response is… that we will give them R700'. They did not have a problem with that.

Then we knocked off and I came back to Johannesburg on Tuesday [14 August]. We received another phone call from SAfm [the country's premier English-language radio station] . We went into the studio, [it was] Wednesday the 15th. It was ourselves, it was the president of NUM, and it was management as well. So all three of us were talking to this issue. I must point out that we are not vilifying anybody. But we must point out that the unions that we have trusted for so long, the unions that have been at the forefront of every aspect of the employees, I do not know what is happening to them. They are definitely failing the employees. I don't know if it is because of the BEE [Black Economic Empowerment] component—they are also owners of these mines. They sit on the board with the owners of these mines. They [NUM] have lost focus and direction to lead and champion the causes of the employees.

Now, the advent of AMCU was to counteract [this process]. AMCU was born in 1999 and it got registered in 2001, and our objectives were clear: that we will not align to any political party, number one. Number two, we will only deal with the issues that affected the workplace and many others, so we have lived to that promise that we made for ourselves… and we are realising that dream that we have set for ourselves… We agreed [at the end of the SAfm discussion] that we will definitely sort this problem, and we will talk to our people, all three parties involved… It was around this time and then we… agreed that we need to come in the morning and speak to the logistics of how people should go back to their posts, and management agreed… that this is going to happen, and we assured the employees that this is going to happen…

Thursday morning, when we arrived at Marikana, it was 20 past 8 in the morning, and we found that the management and the police were [in a meeting]… and they were releasing statements. We waited and waited until half past ten, and it was only then that we were able to speak to the management... [The management now demanded that] the people come down from the mountain and go to their respective posts. And [they said that] we will [only] talk after they have gone back to work. But, now, management—remember, [when] you are not working in the mine and have been absent for five days or so, you need to go for induction, where you are re-orientated, because these guys are driving big machines and they need to concentrate all the time when they are working in all those horrible places—but management said 'No, let them go back to work, we are no longer interested in that, let them go [straight] back to work'... [After a while] we [AMCU] were standing alone. There was no NUM, there was no management, and all of them vanished into thin air. And then our president said: 'Now look at the time, it is now half past two, and we need to go to those people and talk to them, and plead with them that they should... descend that mountain and go back home. We will deal with the situation.'

Unfortunately, when the workers are poised for their demand, then you will not get them to do anything until you bring them what they want. And we tried, as AMCU, and in fact they were now begging us and [they] say: 'Leave now, and we thank you president of AMCU. We have heard you [and] we have seen your leadership and we have seen your people. Now you must leave, and if the police want to kill us then let them find us here.'... And I can tell you... at this point, I don't know, there was some electrical movement... And I want to say to you people, that president Mathunjwa is a kind of a leader who had, I think, he has eight senses. And he said, 'Comrade Mphahlele are we failing to beg these people to disperse... these people from the mountain. I can see that once we leave this place then they are going to be killed.'

... Then the comrade [one of those on the mountain] came and he said [to us]: 'Comrades, it is time for you to leave, and if we die, we will die here,' and we respected that. Then, because that area was infested with every kind of police, every kind of vehicle, we decided that we are not going to go from the front; then we decided to go [past] the police in a back door, that road that leads to Marikana. And on our way we were met, just five minutes from the koppie of horror, we were met with... vehicles of the police... [They were] armed to the T. One gentleman asked from that vehicle: 'Why are you speeding, why are you speeding?' Then the president of AMCU said: 'No I am not speeding, we are driving away from this place.' And he [the police] said: 'Who are you?' And he [Joseph] said, 'We are representatives of AMCU.' And then he [police] said: 'Where are you going? Go back!' And then the president said, 'No, I am going out of this place'. Then one [officer in] the vehicle said: 'Wait. Let us double check'... They called their control room and they spoke to the general, and they said, 'Yes, leave those guys, because they are union officials.' And then after 20 minutes of detention then we were left to go.

When we were in Marikana we were still debating in our minds [whether we should leave]. Then the president said: 'No, let us go back, because, should anything happen to these people, then they will say AMCU ran away.' The president said: 'Let us go back there and die with those people, if that is the call for today.' One of our comrades, the national organiser, Comrade Dumisane, [said]: 'President, I respect that idea, but remember if we perish now with these people, then no one will live to tell the story.' And we drove off. After Dumisane, having said that, the phone rang in the president's phone... It was one of the media people... [and the media] said: 'Comrade Joseph, the people are being killed.' And at that time the video company had a news. They were saying 12 had already died.

The team that came behind [the workers] is the team that started this thing, and when you see people running in front of your TV, they were being chased by the team there, from behind... And if you look at some clips you will see that five of the Nyalas [also referred to as Hippos in workers' accounts] drove the eastern side, and then immediately the razor wire was dropped, and that was closing the distance [to restrict] these comrades to go to their *mkhukhus* [shacks]. And that is why now you saw that those comrades were running towards the police, because they were being shot.

I like horror movies, and I normally watch them, and I thought that maybe these are just films, they are just being made. That is not true. You have seen the truth. People were blasted... and sprayed with guns with bullets. That is where we are.

But in the midst of all this comrades we welcome your support. Therefore, as AMCU, and as much as the president of the country has called an independent commission, what we are calling for [is] an independent and outside body that could deal with the root cause of this matter, because we do not trust the terms of reference. Where are they going to come? From the very same people who killed our people? So we are also advocating for an independent Commission of Inquiry. How can you be a player and a referee at the same time? That cannot happen.

Amandla [power]!

AUDIENCE RESPONDS: Awethu [is ours!]

I thank you comrades!

5

Interviews with mineworkers

**Undertaken by Thapelo Lekgowa, Botsang Mmope,
Luke Sinwell and Bongani Xezwi**

Mineworker 1

MINEWORKER: My brother, I was born in the Eastern Cape...
while I was still learning at school, I told myself that I was not going
back to school the next year, I wanted to go work. The reason why
I wanted to go work was because all my friends were working and
even on Christmas they had money, and whatever I got, I got from
my friends... I told myself that I will not be able to go study anymore
because I saw my friends working and the other reason was that I
wanted to change my life. And even at home it was just my father
only, my mother had already died, so a person's life changes when you
have no mother... and then we spoke with my friends that I will come
in December, that I will come next year, so in December I gave my
ID [identity document] to one of the guys, so that when he goes back
to work they should find me work too. So at home we started with a
flat, two room... and then I came here in Gauteng, and when I came
here I went to Marikana where I started working in Wonderkop...
but when I first got here I went to join the line... and then again...
I was hired, and when I was hired I loved the hostel. And I earned
R1,300 when I first got here and I did not have a problem that I went
there because I was still very young and I did not have many things
to do. And everything I had to do was to make me happy and then
now I enjoyed going on leave as a working person and that made me
very happy.

And in 2003 I came back and then at home my brother and father,
as my father was still alive, they asked me now to get married. And
then I saw that the time for me to get married has not come because I

was still able to go there and there, you see? I was happy about the fact that I was still able to run there and there and then I told myself that, no, I will wait, and then my father died and we then buried him... and then I went back to work and earned a living and I was helping here at home. And then I told my brother that time for me to get married has not arrived because the person who wanted me to get married had died and I was not ready to get married. No my brother said, 'No there is a problem with that'... [about two years later] I told my brother I now wanted to get married and he told me to, 'Go think about that' and I said to him I had thought about it and he still said, 'No go back and think about it some more and then come back.' And then I went back to Wonderkop and then I went back to him again... and I told him that, 'No, I want to get married,' and he said, 'Okay'... and I got married and I took her from her home and brought her to [the] mine and so... I left her at home and I came back to Marikana and so when I got here I worked and in December came time for me to take cows to her home, and then we went on with my wife and we stayed at home and we were happy...

We had a child and the child was a girl and she died. And maybe she was about 4 or 6 months and then again she got pregnant and we got twin boys. And that was not a problem but one died again and one survived, but then when I went back again the other one died again and we also lost another girl. And then I had another two kids on the side because I was still able to run around and then I finally had a child [again]... the place I am in now... I see that I am not short of anything but the only thing I am short on [is] water and streets but another thing is that we have electricity and toilets. And so my life is right now back home, but now the only thing we are short of is streets, just two streets in the rural areas of Ntendele, but other areas around us are short of other things like that... So I should compare life in Marikana and life back home, but life back home is better.

The reason why I say that is because here is a place I work in and I live in a shack, so everything I do that is nice is back home. So a lot of money I get I send it back home, and that will make sure that when I get home I will have a better life and I can sit on a sofa, not here in Marikana... I see which life is better, but the only thing that is bad [where I stay in the Eastern Cape] are the streets because they don't have gravel. It is just mud and when it rains you have to wear gumboots even during the week... So you see, a better life is back home, so even the soil here is not like back home...

INTERVIEWER: Since you started working here in the mine did your health suffer even a bit or what?

MINEWORKER: No, my brother I can't say I suffered in any way... I have nothing to make me suffer because I have a small family, and so my brother was able to support in one place, and so now I saw that it is time for me to get my own place, you see? But I tried to suffer because when I got paid I would give my pay again as it was given to me because we were building a house [in the Eastern Cape]... And that is when I saw that the money I am earning is not enough, like food. I send R3,000, because I want them to eat, maybe use R1,500 to buy more bricks for the house and with the other R1,500 buy food... And on my side I have to pay my instalments... for clothes, so I am forced to go pay... R200 and I take R300... and after I am only left with R500 and when I do buy food then I have to make sure that the food I bought will be enough... Or maybe I used R300 so even if I know that I am suffering, but at least I have food to eat, you see? And so that is where I have a problem and see that my health is suffering.

INTERVIEWER: [What happened during the strike from 11 August 2012, two days after you first met at the stadium?]

MINEWORKER: On Saturday on the 11th, then we decided to go to the NUM offices so that they can tell us what we should do now, because we went to the employer on our own and they [NUM] went and stopped us from talking to the employer, and we wanted them to tell us what to do. On Saturday they [workers] went and when they were still on their way there [workers] were shot by the NUM members, they shot at them... And after we went to them and they shot at us we then went to the mountain, we were sitting at the grounds [Wonderkop Stadium] and while sitting there we saw that the place is not right and then we decided to go to the mountain. And we stayed at the mountain from the 11th after the shooting and the 12th and the

13th and then we sat there again on the 13th and the 14th. And I think on Wednesday [the 15th] the president of NUM came and he was talking to us in a police Nyala, and we told him all we wanted as we were sitting there, and they promised on Wednesday that they will bring the employer to come talk to us and hear what we wanted and that is how we ended things on Wednesday. And that is when Zokwana came and he said he came to tell us to go back to work, and then we saw that he was not speaking about the right thing... and, secondly, he was not in a right place to talk to us as a leader, as our president, this thing of him talking to us while he is in a Hippo [Nyala]. We wanted him to talk to us straight if he wanted to. We wanted him to talk to us so that we will be able to negotiate with him as he is the boss of the ones who shot at us, you see?

So on Thursday we were supposed to get the report to tell us how they went on Wednesday and they did not give us the answer of how they went as they were with police. And then the AMCU people came also and they also said that the employer should give an answer. These people of AMCU went there and came back and told us the employer did not want to speak to him and he has finished whatever he wanted to say now and as he was saying that he also asked us to go back to work because the decision that was taken was not right. So now [he said], 'Please go back to work' and we told him that, 'no one had told us to go there and stay there [at the mountain], and that we went there on our own without any union. We never came here as a member of NUM [or] of AMCU, and the only place AMCU was leading was in Karee only.' And here in Eastern and in Western it [AMCU] was not there, it was only NUM there. And then Zokwana said some things. He said he had no member in the mountain. [He said] his members went to work but that is something we heard on the radio and we did not hear it directly from him and then we told ourselves that no, let's forget about that because the only thing we want is to see the employer.

And the AMCU president tried to beg us to go back to work, and he said that they will stay behind and talk with the employer. And then we told [him], 'No sir we will not hear that from you, because the committee called us here'. And at that time he left and we think he never even got to Marikana before then. And we saw Hippos, and they were joining a wire, barbed wire. And they pulled that wire, the first car, the first Hippo, and the first one ended while we were still sitting there. And then they pulled the second one, and they joined to the other one, where it had ended. After that we thought that 'no, we should move from there', and then we did, and we ran to the other side, and then after that... we started to run because we did not want to be in that yard they were making for us... Many of us ran there [probably towards the remaining gap], and we all met there, and then they started. And on our side we were running, we were not fighting, because we saw that wire. And then we ran, and then they started to shoot, and we did not know how many people died.

But we saw that, the way things were there was no way people would not die because it was an open space there, and then I looked [at] the distance I had to run and I saw the Hippos were [coming] right at us. And I thought that now I had to change direction and go through the shacks, and that is when I saw that the police were doing what they were doing at that time. And at that time the Hippos were chasing people, it was the soldiers' Hippo. And there was another truck with tear gas, no but they started with the water sprays and they changed to the one with green water, and the soldiers were taking people out, and the police were following by foot. And most people died... while they were running to Marikana, and they died by being ran over with cars on the way going to Marikana.

That is when we went separate directions at that time and on the 16th, on the 17th, and that is when our pain showed because, as people, we knew each other and we wanted to go and see if our brother or my friend or someone I was working with [had died] as we knew each other as people. And then we were asking ourselves if so-and-so survived or what and the people [who] you had phone numbers of you called and found out if they had survived and they would say, 'No, I survived'. Phones were going up and down on the 16th, on the 17th, and you were yearning to see each other's faces just to make sure they survived, especially those [who] we did not know their numbers. That day was a very sad day for us, on the 17th. But we did not know who survived because everyone was running to save his life, but when the reports came and we even heard from the radio also... how many people died then and then. You will find out that when they tell you who died and you find that you know that person, and that started to give us so much pain.

We had pain also on the 16th but it was more painful... on the 17th while we were reporting to each other who was left there. So it was very painful because one did not come back and we did not know if he had died or what and we were worried the whole time.... On the 17th we were still asking each other if they had seen so-and-so and then one would say no I have not seen him. And then that is when we started to look in hospitals and in jails and then what they did was give people a list from jail and even in hospital to find out who was where and who was where, you see? And then after we were given that thing we knew who was where and who was in jail and then we saw that now there is something that makes us happy because now we see the one we thought had died was alive, he is [actually] in jail you see. And still because people were in jail, we did not see why they were arrested, so what happened was very hurtful on 16 August.

INTERVIEWER: Many workers here when we look when they march or sing they carry, what do they call these things, the sticks like the spears and so on, what does that mean, why do you carry spears?

MINEWORKER: My brother, what I can say about the spears, the spears and sticks it's that we came with [them] from back home. It is our culture as black men, as Xhosa men, as I am Xhosa, but it is our culture as black men. It is our culture because even back home we have our spears and sticks. Even here, like when I wake up in the morning or I wake up at night... going to look at the cows, when I go look at anything I always have my spear or stick or here at night or when I have to go urinate, because I don't urinate in the house, I go outside and so when I go out I take my stick, I never go out without it. The stick or the spear, so it's our culture, so the reason we still carry it here, like a white man carries a gun when he leaves his house, that is how he was taught, and so sticks and spears... that is the black men's culture.

Mineworker 2

INTERVIEWER: Could you explain to us how you got to be a part of the meeting of the workers that started on the 9th, could you explain a bit about that, from your side?

MINEWORKER: On the 9th we got together as workers because we wanted to fight for our salaries, we wanted to get a raise. We went to Number 1... and when we got there we meet a white person... we wanted to see our employer but the mine security stopped us and they put danger tapes around, and they also told us that the employer heard about our complaint and they are busy talking about it now. And we asked ourselves how they heard about our complaint without us talking to them. They stopped us from going through, and we listened to them and they told us not to go through and we sat there and waited for five minutes, and then they came back again saying we should wait for a further two hours and we waited for that two hours. And then when they came back, an NUM member came back and told us that the employer will not answer us because we did not start with them [NUM]... On Thursday we started by meeting as workers to discuss how we were going to go to Number 1, and then on Friday we meet again as we were told that we did not go to NUM first and so we decided to go to NUM first [on Saturday] and ask for permission from them and also ask for forgiveness that we went to the employer without telling them first.

And we went as workers to the NUM offices but we were shot at by the NUM people and two people died and we ran and they came after us until we passed the ground and they stopped chasing us when we got to the grounds and that is when we came here in the mountain, and we saw that we were beaten and blood has spilled also and our people have died too. And then we came back and we stayed in the mountain and then we decided that when there is a fight a man should also have his own knobkerrie and then we decided to go get our knobkerries and spears and we went back to the mountain again and we slept there until Sunday.

Sunday we woke up, and we told ourselves that we were going to go back to NUM people to talk to them, as they have beaten us, but the mine security fought with us. There were two boers and there was a Hippo too from the police, government police, and we asked them to pass through, and that is what we did. But they just shot at us and we went to them and they ran and then we went on. The security and government people also shot at us and that is when we went back to the mountain, and we stayed at the mountain.

And again on Monday we were told that there are workers who are working at Three Shaft and we went to stop those workers from working, and we just started walking there and we were not singing and when we got there the mine security stopped us and told us that they wanted to talk to us. But there was [a] boer there which wanted to shoot us, but they were able to talk to him and he came down, and when they spoke to us then we told them that we wanted to go and stop those people who were working because we are striking and we don't want anyone working. And they told us that, 'No one is working', and that they will go and take those people out and stop them from working and they asked us to go back. And we asked them to get the employer for us and they agreed, and they told us not to go through the hostel but to go through the forest. And we went through the forest and while walking there we saw a van and Hippo from the government. They came and when they were closer to us we stopped them and they came out of the vans and Hippos and the person we spoke to was Mr Mzoli and he is in charge of the police and there was also a white woman there also.

And they asked us where we are coming from and we told him where we came from and he asked us why we went there and we told him we went to get the workers who were working while we are sitting in the mountain. And he asked if we knew that it is not legal to carry what we had and we said, 'Yes we knew'. And then he asked us to give them to him and we said, 'We are not saying we're not going to give them to you, but we want you to come with us until we get to the mountain and then when we get there we will give them to you because that is where other people are and the people who sent us are there.'

And the white woman said, talking in English, she said, they should take the weapons and if we don't want to give them, then they should shoot us. And the Zulu policeman said he is going to count to ten and after that he is going to tell his police to start shooting at us. And then he started counting 1 and when he got to 2 we started singing and the police were surrounding... there was a Hippo back and front and we were in the middle and we found a small hole to pass on. On that side there were only six policemen and we went through them, and they let us through, and we did not fight we just sang. And when we had gone for about 10 metres from the police, the police started shooting at us, and that is when two police died and two of our members died too, and some were shot and hurt, and they went to hospital. And we called our people to come to us and they did come to us and the police by then had run off. And the police came back with a Hippo and they shot at people and the first person they shot on the other side of the dam. When he went past the dam they shot him and the second one was pointed by the helicopter while running and they killed him in a shack. We came back and we looked for a car and we took these people that were hurt and we took them to hospitals and that was on a Monday.

On Tuesday while [we] were still sitting there in the morning around 8, a Hippo came, a lot of Hippos came, and they stopped there, and a boer appeared and he spoke over a speaker, and he said, 'workers', talking in Fanakalo, 'workers we did not come back to fight but we came to make friendship, and we would like to see your representatives', and then we told them we do not have representatives, and then he said we should pick five men who will come speak to them and they will come back after we have picked them... and when they got there they told us that he did not come to fight but to build a friendship and then they spoke to him and said to him that we want the employer and then they left saying they are going to get the employer on Tuesday, they said they will come back on Wednesday.

And on Wednesday they came back, and they said we came back to build a relationship with you, and they did not want to come out of the Hippo saying it was the rules. When they speak to us they should not come out of the Hippo, and those are government rules. The rule says when a person talks to people they should not come out of the Hippo. And they came back on Wednesday to build a relationship and we told them that we are not going to talk to them, we are waiting for our employers they are going to bring and then they sat there. And around 4pm Mr Zokwana came with a Hippo, and they said they came back to build a relationship with us and we came with your representatives. And then again we went to the Hippo and when we got there we saw Mr Zokwana there, and then we asked them to take the speaker out so that we will talk over it. And then it was clear that they did not want to and then again Mr Zokwana said no, but then again they took it out and we spoke and we said we are thankful that Mr Zokwana is there and we hope that we will reach a solution soon. But Mr Zokwana said he was not there to talk to us, and then he said we should just go underground and if we don't want to then he is going to tell the police to shoot us.

And the Hippo went back and he said he was going to call our AMCU representatives. They left and came back a short while after with AMCU people. The AMCU people also talked and we told them to come out of the Hippo because we don't know them... They told us that here in South Africa the rules say they should not come out while speaking to them while in the Hippo and then we told them that then we have nothing to say to them, we just want them to go get our employer and that they should come back...

[On] Thursday... they came with their own car and the Hippo were so many by then and there were also Hippos with wires in them, the one they used to close there, and we kept going to talk to the boers... and Mr Mathunjwa asked us, and he even went down on his knees and cried, and he said he is begging us to go back to work and they will remain there talking about how we are going to get the money, R12,500. And we said, 'No we cannot do that', and we also asked him to go back because we are not AMCU members, we are not NUM members... But then he left and he just went about 50 metres turn around the stones there, and what happened after that, is that we were closed off with that wire and then we left there and we went over to the [kraal] and that is when they started shooting at us. And the first person who started to shoot was a soldier in a Hippo, and he never shot a warning shot. He just shot straight at us, he shot a person who was wearing a Kaizer Chiefs T-shirt, and that is the first person which fell. He was hit here and he was behind me, and they hit him and he fell and they shot at us while we were there in [the kraal] and they also used tear gas on us, they shot at us until we got there.

People were not killed because they were fighting, they were killed while they were running, we were not fighting, we were shot while running and we went through the hole and that is why we were shot. We did not want to be closed in with a wire like we were cows. And people ran to the mountain, and some were even ran over by Hippos, the soldier Hippos, and that is what happened, and some were shot at and killed with guns and a lot of people were ran over by Hippos.

On Friday [the 17th] the South African President Zuma [came]... He said he will bring his people here to come and kill us and then it was clear to us that he was the one who told his police to kill us... Zuma never came to us... The person who came to us first was Malema. Malema was the first person to come to us and then all the other parties came. And Zuma was the last person to come to us and he said he heard what we are saying. And he has tasked a committee to investigate and find out what the truth was because he said we are thieves as we are liking our spears and that means we had the intention to kill as we are liking our spears. [He said] we are liking people's blood and then from there, the only people who were able to get us to see the employer to talk as we are still talking even today, were the church people and the traditional chiefs from around here. And even traditional chiefs from the Eastern Cape came to mourn with us with the hardships here, as we are still here and days have gone by and we still want the R12,500. And we are saying we are not going underground until we get the R12,500 and we are not going underground while our people are still in prison for fighting for their rights, and we are not going underground until our people are buried and we are not going underground until people are replaced.

As today we are preparing transport to go and bury some other people who are going to be buried this week, and next week we are going to bury people, so that we finish with the burials, and now we still waiting for the people we have sent there as our representatives to talk to our employer. And this thing, people [the media] say that unions are at war, saying that NUM and AMCU are fighting. Those are lies. Here, workers are the ones who are at war. AMCU offices are at Karee and in Eastern and Western are NUM offices. There are no parties fighting, here only workers, workers are fighting for their rights and they want their money and they are being killed by NUM and Zokwana and the mine and the government that we vote for every day.

Mineworker 3

INTERVIEWER: So could you explain to us about the strike and when it started?

MINEWORKER: The strike started on the 9th and that is when we started to meet, on the 9th and when it started on that day it was for the drill operators... and when we went to the management on Thursday... the management did not want to talk to the drill operators... And after the management refused to talk to them, to us, then NUM came to us and told us that management will not speak to us. And that is when we stood there and we did not leave, we refused to leave, so then the second person who came back to us was black from management, not the one we wanted to talk to. He said management heard our complaint and that is when we had a problem because we have not spoken to him yet. Where did he hear about our complaint because we have not told him what we want from him? And the day went by that day, and then there were police by then. They were called there and they told us that we should not be there. [He said] we should leave because if we don't want to go then the police will do their jobs. Then we went back, and by then we heard that NUM said we did not talk to them first as a union, we just went on our own to management.

So we came back and then we decided that people who work night shift, as there are people who work night shift, now everyone as we have come back from management will not go to work because management was showing no respect because they did not want to talk to drill operators. Then the strike was for every worker, and that is when it started. Saturday we decided to go to NUM as they have said we cannot go and talk to management before talking to them first.

But before we even got to their offices they came out and shot at us as workers of Lonmin and two people died on Saturday. And when we left from there we were not able to get inside the stadium, where we hold our meetings because the gates in the stadium were closed. They did not want us there anymore.

And then we decided to go to the mountain because now we see that we are not welcomed there anymore and that NUM shot at us in their offices and then we went to the mountain. We started going to the mountain Saturday when the NUM started shooting at us... We got there and we sat until after the AMCU representative came to us from Karee... He thought he was going to get the employer to talk to [but he could not]. And then he left, and then he came to tell us that the person he got there was not the employer, he was just a person working in that office only, so we sat in the mountain.

On Sunday the police came, and we also decided that we are going to Bop Mine, to tell Bop Mine that there should be no one going to work totally and that they should know that the whole place is closed and at Bop Mine we found police waiting for us there. And near the stadium in Wonderkop they asked us not to go to Bop Mine and it is late now and we agreed and we went back to the mountain, and we stayed there.

Monday [13 August], the police came, and there were many of them, then, with another white man who can speak this language we use in the mine, but he was in the police Hippos. He said he wanted to speak to us and he wants to build a relationship with us. And we tried to get the committee that we choose to go to management, and the management wanted to talk, this man in the car. We said that these men should go there and talk to these people facially [face to face] and they denied to do that and they did not want to come out of the Hippo, they only gave us a speaker. While they were still inside the Hippo, they said they wanted to build a relationship with us. And we asked, 'What kind of relationship because the only thing that made us stay here is that we want to see the employer.' They never wanted to answer us on that. They just said they wanted to, 'Build a relationship with us only'. We said to them, 'Ok now we would like to know your names from you now' and they did not want to give us their names.

And then we told them that, 'We are not going to be able to speak to them anymore then'.

And we went back to the mountain and we stayed there. But they came back again on a speaker saying they wanted to build a relationship with us and we sent our people to go to them again. And then this man said, Mambush said, 'Before I speak to you now, can you give me your names?' And they did not want to. And inside there was a white woman there, and this [other] man we think is the mine boss but only he is wearing private clothes and these bullet proofs underneath... What he did was he took a phone from the workers in the mine and he asked to take a picture of them and they said no and they looked down. They did not want to speak to them, and then they told them that, 'Now because you don't want to give us your names and you don't want us to take a picture, then we will not be able to speak to you now.'

And again on Tuesday [14 August], they [came] back again and then later they were able to go to their homes and again in the morning they came back. They came back still wanting to build the same relationship they wanted to build yesterday and now, no one wanted to speak to them... we asked them to come with us or else they should bring management where we are. [We said] 'Those are the only two things we want from you, either you bring management to us or you take us to management, those two things.' And they said they have nothing that joins them with us. Now they are only there to do their jobs only, they are there to make peace only, they have nothing to do with the fact that we want management and they will not go get management for us...

And again on Wednesday we stayed there and [it became] late. There was still that person that speaks the language we use underground, they call Fanakalo. And [he] still said he wanted to build a relationship with us again, and we said, 'No'. The Hippo they were going with on that day was not the same Hippo they used before. That one had no space to stand and when they spoke to them they were able to step on it and talk to them, but that one had no bumper on it so that they can be able to step on it and talk to them. And they were told to come closer because there was a stone there that would be used to step on and talk to them. And they did not exactly say 'No' but they said these people, the five madoda [men], should come close to them, and the five madoda was able to go to them and then [a worker] stepped in and told them that he had nothing to say to them today if you don't give me your name. While the worker was talking to them he saw this man they say is a president of NUM, Mr Zokwana, and that was on... Wednesday [15 August].

He saw Mr Zokwana and he said, 'Mr Zokwana I am thankful that I am seeing you, please give me the speaker [so] that I [can] speak on it.' But Mr Zokwana said, 'No'. But the white woman there said they should give him, and he said, 'Mr Zokwana I am happy that you came to us, and we plead with you to come out so that we can be able to speak with you.' And Mr Zokwana said, 'No, it is the rule here in South Africa that we should not come out of the Hippo when we speak with you.' And then we said that, 'We do not know that rule as workers because as a leader... where should you come? You should come to the workers and not be on a Hippo.' But, Mr Zokwana said, 'No', and then he took the speaker. Mr Zokwana said to us that, the only reason he came to us, is to tell us to go back underground and there was nothing else he would say to us.

And now all the workers could hear him because he was talking on a speaker they had. And they said, 'No' this person should go because he is not here to help us with what we want, and when he left he said, 'Now I am going and I will call that small AMCU of yours.' And they did call AMCU again. And they were also inside the Hippo and we told them that we are not going to speak to them in the Hippo and they said, 'We are bound by the rules that we found here, but we wanted to come out to you and speak to you outside of the Hippo. But the rules here say we should be inside the Hippo and not come out, because we [i.e. 'you', the workers] are not good people.' And then we said, 'Okay, and we were able to talk to them and found that it is really AMCU representatives, and they told us that they were here to talk to us and we said, 'Okay'. They should talk, there is no problem and when they were starting to talk about how we are going to talk about our issue. And the workers said, 'This has nothing to do with you and if you want to talk to us then tomorrow you should go get the employer here because this has nothing to do with the union. We as workers want the employer only.' And really the AMCU president said to the workers [that he] will go to the employer and [he] will come back tomorrow and [provide us with] the report-back.

And then the following day, I am sure around 12pm, and they told us that the reason they came late is that we had a delay in the meeting... because they said they will be there by 9am and then they told us that there was a delay with the management there. And on that day the unions were all there and we told them that we have nothing to say to them. We said, 'We only wanted the employer', and we asked him to go and tell them that we workers only wanted the employer only and we have nothing else to say to you. We thought that you will be able to bring the employer here only... and there were also soldiers there on that day. We said, because there are soldiers there now, he should come with the soldiers and the police are there also and they will be able to make sure that he is safe there and when he [Mr Mathunjwa] went back to the mine offices of the management, he was not welcomed anymore... the only thing they told him is that our time in the mountain was over, that is what he got from the management offices. [They told him that] their [the workers'] time in that mountain is over because that mountain is under government.

And then he came back to us to tell us that the only thing he got from the office was that our time in the mountain is over and they were going to bring the security people and the police and he said to us men [that], 'The management has finished with you [workers] and now they will spill your blood here.' And he really did plead with us to go from that place [the mountain] because they have already signed about us in that place. And we told them, 'No, because you don't [know] anything about this thing here. Then you should go.' And Mr Mathunjwa did just that. And I am sure after ten minutes after he left, the police spread out the wire. There were trailers that had that wire and then they spread the wire and after that... they started to shoot at us. And while they were shooting at us we could not run to the shacks where we live, we could only run towards the front there and that side was already closed off...

But after the soldiers arrived, that is when they used that wire and they have used the wire before and we asked them to take the wire off and they agreed to that. And after the soldiers arrived with the two Hippos the police said they will not take that wire out and they will go on with doing their jobs, and that is when we got hurt. Like me, I was able to save myself because when I ran I ran to this side and a lot of people who got hurt ran towards that mountain there. Those are people who got hurt the most, they ran towards that kraal there and some were left behind here and some were taken by soldiers going towards that mountain. What happened in that mountain, god knows, because by then they were using that green tear gas, bluish like the sky because that mountain was green. What happened in that mountain I cannot say because I was very far by then and the helicopter was shooting at us too and that went on like that on Thursday on 16 August.

INTERVIEWER: Can you tell me about the five madoda and the committee?

MINEWORKER: You see my brother, the five madoda, the word used by the police, they said they wanted the five madoda, that is the language they used. And that is the language we use in the mines, but they were using police cars, so that name five madoda was given to us by the police. The time they wanted to talk to us, and really we did that, we choose the five men, as now they are called five madoda, but they were there ones who gave us that name, because they wanted to speak to only five people, they did not want to speak to all of us.

[We chose them] on that day [probably the 14th, possibly the 13th]. The committee, you see was very big at that time. And they were there ones in front of us, and we choose these men [the five madoda]. We [already] had a committee [before then]. The committee made sure there was peace and order, and they were looking after us. We already had that committee, only it was not just the five madoda. When you go on a strike you have people who are able to control people; not to do, as other strikes [do when] people mess up and damage stores and beat people, things like that. So those people were able to control people in that way. It was the first time [we had this committee] because the union that we thought will represent us, did nothing for us. Then we thought that we should choose some members from our workers to do that, because the union was not doing their jobs anymore.

Mineworker 4

INTERVIEWER: How long has this struggle been on-going?

MINEWORKER: This struggle is of Lonmin in its entirety, what we wanted was money. We were not fighting. I heard management say that we were fighting the unions. We were not fighting the unions, we just wanted money: R12,500.

INTERVIEWER: Which union?

MINEWORKER: NUM. Yes... we were not fighting them, they were the ones who shot at us on Saturday morning at our residence and we ran away...

INTERVIEWER: Who shot at you in the residence on that day?

MINEWORKER: It was the union leaders, the union committee. They were the ones who shot at us, they killed two boys. We ran and left them there. Even the mine security guards were shooting, but not at us. They were shooting upward in order to scare us and we ran away and left for the mountain. When we tried to go to them on Sunday [12 August], the mine security guards shot at us. But we did not go back. We kept going forward. As we proceeded forth, we met more mine security guards who also shot at us. We continued on and that's when they caught those boys, beat them but they did not kill even one of them. When we came back, the union representatives were already gone and I went up to the mountain. I think it was on... [Thursday, 15 August] there arrived soldiers and the police. When they arrived there, they put up a wire fence. We tried to stop them and [they] said that we should not try to stop them, that they were going to do what they came here for. Okay... we left them... we told them not to put up the fence because we were not destroying anything. They stopped.

There [they] arrived, our leaders from AMCU [and they] spoke to us. One guy said that it seemed as if [we] went underground [then] they were done, they were going to kill us and that he wanted all the members alive and none of them injured. Then we said that there was no way that we would go back to work without getting that money in our hands. There is no money and we have been struggling for a long time. I want money, our children are struggling at school... On Thursday morning, these people arrived again and they put up a fence and we tried to stop them and they stopped. Then there arrived AMCU leaders and [they] said to us that they were going to speak to our management and would be back in a little while and that we shouldn't leave as yet. They did indeed go, but when they got there, the management of the company was not available. They came back to give us that report and then they left. After about 20 minutes, there came soldiers with their cars. When they arrived, they took out guns and shot us. There was confusion there, and some people were run over by Hippos. Shots were also being fired from helicopters. I am not sure what happened thereafter, I just saw many bodies being picked up. Yes... even today we say that we want that money R12,500, nothing else. We weren't striking, we just wanted that money.

INTERVIEWER: Were you also there when they killed those people?

MINEWORKER: Yes, I was there sir.

INTERVIEWER: So how did you survive that day?

MINEWORKER: I lied on the ground when they shot, because if you stood up they said that you were going to get hurt. I was crawling and then proceeded to lie on the ground, and that was how I survived... by crawling on the ground and lying down flat. I crawled out of the scene and ran to a nearby shack...

INTERVIEWER. Where did the other people run to?

MINEWORKER: Others ran to Marikana and those who ran to Marikana were shot at the most, even from helicopters. Others were run over by Hippos. It is not everyone who was shot at, others were stepped on by Hippos....

INTERVIEWER: Is there anything else you want to tell me, perhaps a question that I did not ask you?

MINEWORKER: I can say that what happened... we were killed for nothing. They were fighting us for our money. We were not fighting with management. We simply wanted to know when they were going to give us our money. Management thought it was better for them to call the government to come and kill us. There was something else going on there. No one can just kill without authority. There must have been a deal between our management and NUM... there was definitely a deal, because we were told to go underground. We won't go underground until we get that money, R12,500. No one is striking, we only want that money. If they can come and give it to us now, we will go back to work. That's it, there is nothing else. We just wanted management to say, 'On such and such a date, we will give you your money,' but instead, they fetched those police to kill us while we were not striking.

INTERVIEWER: I heard you say that some members of NUM killed workers at the mine residence. Have there previously been clashes between NUM and the workers or between NUM and AMCU? Do you know anything about that?

MINEWORKER: Listen sir, this is how the story goes... when the workers went that side to tell them that we wanted more money, we found that NUM had not confronted management about this issue. So, we told them that we could see that they were unwilling to help us, so we will go to management ourselves because we were the ones who were suffering, and they were just sitting comfortably and drinking tea. When they got to their office they found us there and [NUM] asked us why we had gone above their heads. They told us that nothing will go well without their support. Then on Saturday morning they [NUM] went there wearing their red shirts and they shot people. They shot two people... this was on Saturday morning when this strike began. Some of us ran away, there was nothing else that we could do... We wanted to run to the stadium but people were being shot there, so we went to the mountain instead... we would have held our meetings there [in the stadium] if they were not killing us...

INTERVIEWER: Were any of the workers in possession of guns maybe?

MINEWORKER: No, none of the workers had guns. Some were holding swords in case of snakes, so that they would be able to defend themselves, also some firewood to make fire. If there were workers with guns, then I did not see them. Yes, we only had swords. We have been struggling while the union leaders were comfortable, drinking tea. When they have a problem, the management helps them quickly. Even their cell phones are always loaded with airtime, R700, R800, while we are struggling. This strike is not a union and workers' strike, but the workers demanding money from management. We only want money from management. The union was not involved, AMCU was not involved either because they found the strike on-going. We only just wanted money. There is nothing else, just that R12,500. If they can give us that money tomorrow, tomorrow we will go back to work. This money is too little, and we can't make ends meet with it...

INTERVIEWER: How much do you earn per month?

MINEWORKER: I earn R4,000, but it does not last. Children must go to school, and when they go to school, they need some lunch money, and books are expensive. The children are really struggling... we don't have enough clothes... we are really struggling. The workers of Lonmin are really struggling, but we work very hard. You will hear that the stocks are up, but we get nothing. This company rates number three among the platinum mines, but we are not getting anything. The company is well off, but the workers are not well off... These machines don't make us money; we work hard, but get nothing in return. The white people reprimand us if we do not do our work properly or make a mistake. It would have been better to be reprimanded knowing that we were getting better pay. The white people pay each other better, but we get nothing.

Mineworker 5

INTERVIEWER: According to your view, how are the conditions that you are working under?

MINEWORKER: The conditions in the mines are those of oppression, you find yourself pressured to reach the set target. If you haven't reached that set target for the day, then you can't knock off and go home.

INTERVIEWER: How many hours do you work from day to day?

MINEWORKER: According to the law we are supposed to work 8 hours, but we don't work for 8 hours. We work for 12 hours and even 13 hours... After that, you are occupied with work but get unsatisfactory pay even after working for all those hours...

INTERVIEWER: So what were your union leaders saying about these conditions that you are working under?

MINEWORKER: These unions did not cover us according to their function, because when we took our complaints to them, they did not seem to take them seriously, that is when we decided that this time, we would overtake the unions, we ended up wanting this as workers. It was then that it seemed as though the unions were fighting us as the workers, then this upheaval continued...

INTERVIEWER: Were you there on the day when many workers were killed?

MINEWORKER: Yes, I was there sir... I arrived there at around about 8:30am, the police with their many cars arrived at about 9am. When they arrived, they put up a wire fence so we tried to stop them from doing so, telling them that there was no need to put up a fence because no one was fighting, that the only thing that we wanted was the R12,000. They stopped putting up that wire fence, and there arrived some people from AMCU and we talked to them. [We were] telling them that we refuse to leave until we get the R12,000 or get an employer who will tell us what they say about us now that we were sitting out in the field, having left the company building because we were chased away by the union. We were chased out of the stadium by the union because it was killing the workers. Then that person [from AMCU] told us that he was going to call the employer, thereafter he told us that the head of the police with whom he was communicating telephonically could no longer be reached on the phone.

Then after that representative from AMCU left, the police put up a fence, we tried to leave that place because we saw that the fence was meant to keep us in... That was when they tried to stop us from leaving and other workers died and some of us were able to escape... Those of us who were arrested, we were not taken to the police station, we were detained within the mine, in a place called B3. When we got to B3, our fingerprints were taken, our pictures were taken, and then we were taken to the police station... This taught us that that the company possibly has their own police force... It seemed as though the police did not belong to the government, but that they belonged to the company... We did not all go to the same police station, others went here and there, others went to Phokeng. I went to Phokeng police station where some of us were beaten and mistreated. We ended up crying in court and we were taken to jail in Mogwase. As you see me now, I came from Mogwase and came here to you today. That is how the story went.

INTERVIEWER: Is there any other thing that you can tell me pertaining to that day, a question I did not ask maybe?

MINEWORKER: No sir, there is nothing else. Those were the only things which I saw unfold on that day... because they removed us from there to here and the police were saying, 'Right here we have made many widows' while they were removing the bodies. It was late in the afternoon.

INTERVIEWER: What were they saying?

MINEWORKER: They said, 'Right here we have caused women to become widows. We have killed all these men'. It was the police who spoke in that manner...

INTERVIEWER: Were the police speaking in that manner?

MINEWORKER: The police were speaking in that manner. Even at the police station in Phokeng, we were asked why we wanted R12,000 because we were uneducated.

INTERVIEWER: Tell me, how were the conditions in detention, how long were you in jail?

MINEWORKER: [We] were arrested on... the 16th and left on Thursday of the 20 something... It was on Thursday when we were taken to Mogwase because our case was postponed to the 6th... We were badly treated... we couldn't eat nor phone our families to tell them where we were. As a person with TB, I was unable to take my medication. I was unable to call my children. I even told the police that I was a widower, and my children were left by themselves... I couldn't tell my children where I was.

INTERVIEWER: Where were you sleeping?

MINEWORKER: We slept on the cement floor... that is how it was.

INTERVIEWER: Tell me, I understand that people were killed from this kraal, when the police were saying that they had made widows... people including yourself ran towards those rocks over there... were there others who ran in this direction?

MINEWORKER: Like I said, everyone was running to safety. I did not really see if people ran this direction or not. It was when I was on those rocks that I noticed that some had run in to the nearby houses, but I couldn't see them very well because I was already hiding... I was arrested because I was hiding. You were shot at if you put up your hands.

INTERVIEWER: So you did not put up your hands?

MINEWORKER: I did not put up my hands. I was taken by a gentleman who was of Indian ancestry. He held me and when I tried to stand up I was hit with guns and he stopped them... He stopped them and that was how my life was spared.

Mineworker 6

MINEWORKER: I am originally from [the] Eastern Cape, I work for Lonmin. I started working here in 2001... After completing Grade 12 I came to work here in Lonmin. I was raised by a single parent, my mother who was not married. I have two brothers and three sisters back home. I am a second born after my sister. I am followed by four siblings which makes a total of six children. When I arrived here at

Lonmin they were looking for unskilled labourers with no working experience and that is how I got hired. I left home because I had hopes of starting my own family but lacked the financial capabilities to do so. Unfortunately, I could not pursue my education due to a lack of financial capability, but I had wanted to make sure that my siblings did not suffer the same fate. I helped my older sister pursue her studies. She matriculated but unfortunately failed in University, another one dropped out in Standard 8. In 2006 I decided to take a wife and made it official... [in] 2006. After that I had to make sure that no one suffered the same fate of not continuing their studies further. Although I was not satisfied with the money I was earning I made sure that my wife furthered her studies in teaching, so that we could meet each other half way and help each other.

... Getting married was not the only dream I had. I also wanted to build a home for myself and my family. South Africa is a democratic country but we as mineworkers are excluded from this democracy. For one, a white person here in the mines gets a better pay than a black person and they are more eligible for promotion and that oppress[es] us black people more. Because when such positions are announced if you as a black person go to apply for the job they ask for a lot of things while they give the positions to white boers from the farms. This is a main reason that is preventing me from realising my dreams...

INTERVIEWER: How would you describe the working conditions here in Marikana?

MINEWORKER: The conditions I work under in Lonmin are not good at all. Firstly, they always make empty promises and they never deliver on them. Secondly, it has become clear that the employer cares more about production than the safety of the workers. If you start questioning about safety our superiors feel that you are stubborn and influencing other members to start asking a lot of questions.

INTERVIEWER: What kind of position do you hold at present?

MINEWORKER: I operate the winch... as far as the union goes, the union which represents us at present has not represented the workers' needs at all, it cares more about the agreements it makes with our employer... I am not satisfied at all about the way the union is representing us because it does not represent the workers' needs, it does what it is told to do, but in terms of having the workers' best interest at heart it has proven incapable of doing so. They side with the employer more than with the worker.

INTERVIEWER: What is [it] that maybe you have done or tried to do differently since you have been a member of this union?

MINEWORKER: As a member of NUM in terms of issues that affect us as workers I approached them with the problems that we workers face and I asked them if an opportunity to further my studies was to ever arise to inform me, all I got from that was that if I wanted to further my studies I should do that and come back with my certificates to get my reimbursement, I did that with my own money and came back to show them but a year has passed since then and I haven't received anything. As a result of this I had to drop out of completing some of the courses because I could not afford to pay for them, this is what I got from being a member of the union.

INTERVIEWER: What did the union do to try and support you or its members in some of the things they also wanted?

MINEWORKER: When it comes to workers' needs, the union makes promises but never delivers on them, and we end up losing a lot. For instance, if maybe your child is sick and you go and approach the union they will ask for a medical report that confirms that your child was really sick. Even if you produce this the employer still denies permission to go and when you approach the union about the matter they don't do anything to address... the issue and this not only affects us physically but also mentally as well.

INTERVIEWER: Would you briefly explain how did you know about the meeting on the 9th and how did you become part of the meeting?

MINEWORKER: On the 6th of August 2012 workers from Rowland Shaft, reel operators, approached the manager with the aim to complain about dissatisfaction over wages. The manager's response was that he does not deal with wage issues, a person responsible for that is at LPD [Lonmin's central office for the whole Marikana complex]. Indeed, on the 9th of August, Woman's Day, workers had a meeting, the reel operators, at Wonderkop stadium. The meeting involved all Lonmin workers from Western, Eastern [and] Karee mine. Their aim was to come up with way a forward. They all agreed that on the 10th of August 2012 on a Friday they all agreed to approach the person who was responsible for salaries of the workers. On their way there near LPD where the employer was situated they were stopped by police who declared the march illegal.

Some people got R300, R900 a month which had to sustain an entire family for a whole month. This also included taking children to school which becomes a problem because most parents cannot afford to take their children to school with the same salary, but our employer did not want to hear any of this and that is where things ended. The reel operators came back and announced that all Lonmin workers will not go to work on the 10th because of the dissatisfaction over wage. The employer sent someone on his behalf saying that he will only speak to the union which represented the workers. On the 11th the workers then decided that they would go and speak to NUM. That is where two workers were shot dead in Wonderkop [taxi] rank and two were badly injured. That is what fuelled the workers' anger. To make things worse they refused the workers [entry] to the stadium.

INTERVIEWER: Were you also part of the march when NUM started firing guns?

MINEWORKER: I was also part of the march. As I was about to enter the gate they started firing at us, but I was fortunate I was not in the front. As soon as they started firing the guns I turned back and we all took cover. Unfortunately, that is where two people lost their lives and others got injured.

INTERVIEWER: Before the meeting on the 9th would you care to explain what was discussed in the meetings leading to the 9th?

MINEWORKER: The workers wanted one thing and that was a better pay, and [we also] wanted representation from NUM but this relationship was destroyed when they started shooting at the workers. The aim was to speak to the employer but this resulted in a lot of dispute and unnecessary conflict, workers ended up saying that we wanted nothing to do with the union any more.

INTERVIEWER: How did the worker's decide on the 12,500 pay?

MINEWORKER: The decision was influenced by the fact that if I am earning R4,000 and I want to get 5,000 we knew if we demanded such a small amount we will only get R200 more, so we decided to demand a higher amount of money so that even if we do not get that we would at least still get a considerable amount, the majority of the workers decided on the 12,500 amount.

INTERVIEWER: Would you briefly explain when and how the committee that represents the people was chosen.

MINEWORKER: As the people who were part of the dispute we decided to elect a committee. People nominated the people who they believed were suitable for certain positions and who would lead us. The committee is representative of all cultural constituencies, it had to be made up of people coming from different provinces.

INTERVIEWER: Would you briefly explain on the 9th where did the workers meet and what did they talk about, similarly on the 10th where did they meet and what did they discuss and what happened [between the 11th and the 16th]?

MINEWORKER: On the 9th, RDOs from Lonmin met at Wonderkop stadium. When they got to the stadium they were denied access by NUM leaders, they filled the stadium with water to restrict access to the people. The workers were requested to elect ten people that will represent them. To go back on the 2011 wage issue workers decided to elect ten people that would go and speak to the employer but when these people got there they were threatened that they would lose their jobs if they continued with the strike which compelled the workers not to elect committees any more. On the 10th a decision was taken that all RDOs in Lonmin will go and speak to the employer because we believed that it would not be easy to fire all RDOs than it would be if we elected five ordinary people, which will make it easier for the employer to fire those people. If we elected another five people he would do the same because he would be trying to block our plan.

On the 11th, RDO workers from Western, Eastern and Karee in Wonderkop were chosen to go to the employer and we took a decision if they failed to address the issue of dissatisfaction over low wages, the workers... [would] go to NUM offices situated next to the Wonderkop [taxi] rank to speak to the leaders. That is where two people were badly injured and the other two died on the scene. On the 12th the workers went to the NUM leaders. On their way there they were shot at by Lonmin guards. Workers realised that this situation was beyond their own hands now. They tried running away but some also tried fighting back which led to the death of some of the securities.

On the 13th... on a mountain in Wonderkop, while sitting there the police arrived [and] they said that they wanted to build peace with us... [we said] we do not want anything from you, all we want is our employer. The police left in the evening, they came back on the 14th [and] they said the same thing, that they came to build peace. Workers asked them how so because we told you already all we want is for you to bring the employer here. They said they came to ensure order which was different from their initial statement of building peace. Workers were getting impatient and irritated, more police kept on coming in which was a bit alarming considering that they initially said they wanted to build peace. They started parking Hippos [and] it became clear that police has different intentions. [On] the evening of the 14th, President Zokwana came. He was in a Hippo [and] he instructed us to go back to work. The workers said we have nothing to say to you, you must come tomorrow morning.

On the day of the 15th, the president of NUM, Zokwana, did not come back. Instead we saw president of AMCU Joseph Mathunjwa who was escorted by the police. He said that he was sympathetic of what we as workers were going through. He warned us that since he was also denied access to speak to our employer and although he was not directly involved in the strike, but because he also had members at Karee, he said he will try our employer again the following day. Still on the same day we saw soldiers and police come back again, soldiers pointed what seems to be a gun at us which was covered by a cloth so we could not see it properly. We didn't take much notice of this and they left. On the day of the 16th Hippos started coming in. The soldiers came back in their Hippos [and] the workers decided to go to them and ask what their intentions were, because we were not bothering anyone—'All we want from you is [to] bring us the employer'. The police said we only came here for one reason, to tell you to clear up this area. The workers asked who sent them there. They said their boss William Phembe sent them there. We asked if they could give us telephone numbers which we could contact...

After that they started putting up a razor fence that separated them from the workers, upon which the AMCU president warned us that we were going to be killed, a decision taken by the NUM. Workers said they would not go back to work until the employer came to speak to them, otherwise this would be all a waste of time. After he [the president of AMCU] left we saw media pack up their equipment. [A] few minutes after that we saw a person come out of the Hippo who seemed to be a leader preparing to go to war. After that he called the police and said 'Red' and started shooting at the workers. They started bringing the Hippo closer to [us and] stamped on the workers that were already injured. There were also helicopters about ten of them that were also shooting at the workers. We ran away but the entire mountain was surrounded by police, some of the police were on horses which is one of the main reason that led to the death of so many workers on that day. 259 people were arrested on the 16th, accused of killing the police. On the 17th the surviving workers met again to see how many people were still alive and to go forward with our mission of getting [the] 12,500 increase.

Mineworker 7[1]

INTERVIEWER: And how did you get involved in mining basically?

MINEWORKER: In mining? Okay, it was 2008, when I got here, back from school, from finishing Grade 12; I came here to the mine in search of work. So, we queued in many places... And then from... there were people who employed, so it was a contract, and then they

---

1   Mineworker 7 is a woman.

employed us there, in 2008, and we worked, and we worked for that contract, eh, in the mine, I mean, it was under [contracted to] the mine... So, 2009 our contract changed to the mine, from 2009 up until now, I am still working for the mine today.

INTERVIEWER: And what work were you doing?

MINEWORKER: It's a general work.

INTERVIEWER: And how much did you make at that point, if you don't mind?

MINEWORKER: By the time I was with the contract, maybe it was R3,000-something. But, still, when I went to the mine it did not change. So, I think the contract was better 'cause it was a contract. Now, in the mine, when we went to the mine it just got bad.

INTERVIEWER: How much are you making now?

MINEWORKER: Eh, it's still R3,000, but it ranges from rank to rank. The contract is more than the mine, you see, so...

INTERVIEWER: What does that mean, it got bad, like it got bad?

MINEWORKER: I mean, when I went to the mine I thought it would be a change in my life, you see? But still, the contract I was with was better than the mine... With the contract you... like sometimes they say, when you are done with your work, go home. You see, it's not as hard work as here with the mine, you see. But still, mine money is less than contract money. So, I don't understand that thing, that is why I was saying 'It got bad', you see.

INTERVIEWER: So, the working conditions for, like,... how are the conditions within which you work?

MINEWORKER: Yho! Ha! Like, it's not safe, not at all. Sometimes there's this thing called 'safety in the mine' yes. But, I don't think it works. Because, sometimes, you find that the place where you must work is not safe. And when you start saying 'safety, safety, safety', they get busy, they say 'what should we do, should we not take out the stove because of your safety?' What should we do, should we not take out the stove, and just sit here because you do not want to be hurt, you see? But, when you come into the mine they just start with safety, they start with safety, but when you're inside there is no such thing; surely our working conditions are bad, and we work painfully, hard, and long hours. But, ah! There's nothing, surely, that we say no, you see.

INTERVIEWER: So, are there any health concerns that you have since you work the mine, or since before the mine?

MINEWORKER: Yho. Working in the mine, there is no one who is not sick working in the mine, they are lying. Because, most of the time, yes, you work bent so, you see? So most of the time you work bent so, and you work bent down for many hours… they do not even give you time to eat lunch, they just say your lunch box must remain on the surface, you see, sometimes when there is a lot of work, sometimes they give you a lot of work when the inspectors are about to arrive. Isn't it that they know that in their job there should be safety measures in place all the time? So, you, you must pretend as if everything is okay to the inspector's satisfaction, yes, something like that. And my back is very painful, my back is very painful, you see.

It is this back. Is it not that I am constantly working hard, I am always bent, I am always this and that. Yes, I do have medical aid, yes, but even it, sometimes they say, maybe, it has no more money, yes. At those times you must take out of your own money. Sometimes your arms are so painful they cannot work, you see. So, that is why I go to the doctor every month.

INTERVIEWER: Do you think, by any chance you can give us a description of your expenses from what you get?"

MINEWORKER: My expenses? As I said, I have siblings, my mother remarried, yes. That man who raised me, who is not my father, I will not abandon him. So, each and every month from this R3,000, I make sure that R1,500 [I] forward home. Fortunately I do not rent the place I stay at, it was my father's house, my biological father. So, this R1,500 goes home and then maybe, plus minus, R600 for groceries and the rest, I mean the rest, R300 for the doctor, it is obvious, it is just obvious, it is just put aside, and then what is left is pocket money. You do not even see that it is pocket money, I do not immediately appear like an employed person, something like that.

INTERVIEWER: Do you ever participate in union activities?

MINEWORKER: Mhm! Ya! But, is it not that when you come to the mine, yes, you must have a union. That is a sure case, you must have a union, and then, we, when we got to the mine, yes, we were given no choice. In fact, we did not know what unions are, what they are for, yes. So, we just fell into this union... they call it NUM... They put us into a union because when you work in a mine you must have a union. Here then is the National what-what of what-what.

INTERVIEWER: And do you have any active participation, that you have when you are in the meetings?

MINEWORKER: No. Like, there would be a lot of people there, you see, so... and... they don't give us a chance, you see. They, if maybe they have an issue that they want to address, they just address the issue, and then end up having no agreement between the people and the leaders, you see, and then the meeting ends just like that. And then when they come back, they come back with decisions.

INTERVIEWER: [What are] your hopes for the future, and your fears?

MINEWORKER: Oh, my fear! So, since we are women, and there are not a lot of women at work, sometimes you cannot even show up at these strikes, because they will spot you early, that: 'Okay, this one attends strikes, I know her, I work with her in the group'. When you get to the mine, they fire you. So, my fear is that, that is why now I do not go to meetings, I do not attend anything, I am scared of being fired from the mine. Should I be fired from the mine where will I go? I will not go anywhere, you see, because I have no parents, like I do not have the parent that worked for me. And the parent that is there now, they depend on me, you see. Then my hopes are that maybe our cries will be heard at last, I do not know, that is the hope we harbour.

INTERVIEWER: Do you think you can tell us your knowledge of the strike that is actually taking place now here in Marikana?

MINEWORKER: So, there were few females there yes. So, I did not stay too long, I just got there, and we did not get those who were at the mountain, we just saw that there were no women and we ended up turning back... Okay we stayed then, until the time of the shooting and so on, you see, then after the shooting, women started attending meetings at the mountains, yes. But I did not frequent the place because most women who went there were unemployed, most of them. The people who are working, it's not that they do not want to go there. It's because they are afraid, because there was a strike last year in May, that strike led to the sacking of many women 'cause they attended it, and many women are known... So, if they see you at the strike, obviously you are gone. So, I think, women have the fear that even this time that could happen, and that is why they do not attend the strike. So I too, I have not attended, I attend it sometimes, you see?

INTERVIEWER: Can you tell us, just, the time you were going to the mountain, as employed women, and then you decided to turn back, or you decided not to end up at the mountain? What was the reason behind that?

MINEWORKER: Oh, as I said, when the strike started... yes, there weren't a lot of women. Sometimes, when you are amongst many men, you end up feeling, no, you see, and truly, there was no reason like what you see. I just saw that there were not a lot of women, and so I just turned back too. That was my reason.

INTERVIEWER: Do you know the committee that... the workers' committee that was elected to speak for the workers?

MINEWORKER: Where we were at the mountain? Yha, people there just, it is like we do not all speak at once, is it not, but we do all sing at once. So, we... they decided that there be people elected to go, to go and talk about what is happening, ya. So, you were not being elected because you are a who's-who, and have what-not, or maybe that you are feared, you see. They elected people who are known for their negotiation abilities, people who, like, their temper, their temper is not short, so that should they talk to people, and there is no agreement, they fight with people. So, people were elected then, and then...

INTERVIEWER: Are there women in this committee?

MINEWORKER: There are not. There is one reason, the one I gave. Sometimes, at these, at the elections, yes, is it not that you would go and deliberate about this and that, and then you go meet with, like, you meet with... let's say they say today you will meet the employer, yes, is it not that you would be present as a woman, the employer will be there too with his people, definitely there will be people who know you there. As I said that there is a fear that they will be sacked even this time. That is why women were never elected.

INTERVIEWER: So, are you saying women are absent from this committee because they are afraid?

MINEWORKER: Eh! They are afraid.

INTERVIEWER: If they were not afraid they would have been elected?

MINEWORKER: They would have been nicely elected. If they had not been scaring us with 'You will be fired, you will be fired'.

INTERVIEWER: When we talk about, uh, the fear of women of being, uh, fired, because they are going to be fired... who fires women and on which grounds?

MINEWORKER: Okay. Is it not that we are working now... we are working. For sure there is a group leader, there is a miner, there is this and that. These people know each other, these people with better positions. These people who work with people, they fire people simply because they want to end up trustworthy, to be trustworthy. I am not saying they are informers or something. It's just that they [are] too just... I am sure that the mine employer does not know my face. Why should he elect to fire me? Of course it's someone who knows me who pointed at me and said, 'I know, there she is, I work with her. The person, the mine employer, does not even know my face. So, definitely sure that the person who knows me at that strike is a person I work with, you see, something like that.

INTERVIEWER: Thank you, sisi.

Mineworker 8

MINEWORKER: Because I had no money and that is when I started looking for piece jobs and I worked... at the clothing store and then I ended up here in the mines in 2006...

INTERVIEWER: When you started working here in the mine, what made you come work here or like how did you get here in the mine?

MINEWORKER: You see my brother, it was not my dream to come work here in the mine but looking at my situation at home, and I was desperate looking for work and so I ended up coming here in the mines... in fact here in the mine, really, really qualifications don't work when they hire you, the only thing that works is money, you have to pay someone to get the job. You bribe someone... yes here in the mine there is place where you find a lot of miners who were long working here and they tell you where to go, and tell you what to do and they guide you that if you have money then you will get the job, and then you bribe someone, and then you do it then... I never told myself that I will work in the mine as I said before I was desperate and then I ended up there, I ended up throwing myself in the mines... what I realised when I got there that first day I got to the mine, I stayed in the mine and then the situation started changing, I saw that my life was not the same, now I was staying with men and I saw all kinds of bad influences and I was regretting being there, and then I went to the mine underground and I did not like it one bit and I thought I was not going to go back there again and they tried to talk to me and they said I should stay strong and I did until now [and it is] 2012...

In fact when I was in school, still studying at school, my dream, and even my father knew that when he was still alive, he knew I wanted to be a doctor, you see? Then he died, then I started suffering there and there in terms of finance, financial, and then I ended up going to places that I did not like.

... The mine has a lot of danger because when you first get there, and when you go in it is just stone everywhere up and down and on the sides and then the air again, the air we inhale is artificial... then there is dust also and we have chemicals that we use there, you see?

And then there is no safety, I cannot say there is 100 per cent safety in the mine because accidents are easy to happen in the mine because the stones there can fall at any time and get on top of a person and even the tools we use are also dangerous and, second, the dust has its own effect too. Now you will find that there you... and that in turn causes TB and then again you have to go to hospital. And then the mine when you do get sick they don't want you to go to an outside hospital, they want you to go to the hospital in the mine and I think that is where they lack to care for people and then they will tell you that, no you have AIDS and things like that, because a lot of people get sick because they work here in the mine and they say they have AIDS when they are sick, and so I don't know how they do that, but there is a lot of risk in the mine, a lot of risk, and every day we see a lot of accidents.

INTERVIEWER: So how [do] you address the issue of safety in the mine, of the accidents in the mine?

MINER: Yes, but they are trying, to improve that thing of safety underground, but the mine will never change... the problem that causes accidents in the mine is pressure, we work under a lot of pressure from our bosses because they want production and then there is also intimidation. They want you to do things that are sub-standard and if you don't want to do that and follow the rules... they say they will fire you or beat you, things like that... the one I can tell you about is this one man, and he was our safety representative, he got hurt in the leg, his leg got cut off, and I think it was 11:30 maybe 10 in the morning... the year was 2008, and that is when his leg was cut off, because he did not want to work in that place and then they forced us to work and they said if we don't want to then they will charge us, this and that and then that man ended up getting hurt...

Mostly in the mine our bosses they hide these accidents, when an accident happens they hide it and then they have stories, they create a story after you are hurt. They say no you hurt yourself, and you know the rules and in the meantime they were the ones influencing you to do it by using intimidation. But when you get hurt they tell stories and say you hurt yourself, and they will hide that and they will make sure it does not get to the government.

INTERVIEWER: Except for this strike, before which union were you under?

MINEWORKER: I was under NUM... It was 21 May, that is when we were supposed to get money for the shares here in the company as mineworkers. We all had to receive that money as mineworkers and I don't know how they invest but we were told that they have invested the money in the bank, and it was invested for five years and after five years we will get that money as workers here in Karee. Karee is another branch here in Lonmin as you see that it is big and we have units. In the Karee unit... and then we on 28 May last year we found out that our chairperson was suspended and we did not know why and what was the problem and then we went on strike and we did not want to go to work but we asked first from our manager, the branch manager. We went to our manager here in Karee to support us and call the people from the NUM region to come and talk to us and explain why they suspended our chairperson and our employer never did that and we went on strike, I think for five days and then after five days people from the NUM region came and they went to the employer and told him to fire us because we do not want to work. And the employer did not waste any time and they fired us.[2]

And after that they re-employed us again at that time and that is when we said we did not want NUM at Karee and we tried to find another union and our manager gave us a right to join any union that we wanted to join if we did not want to be with NUM any more, you see? And then that is when AMCU came to Karee and then we joined AMCU in Karee and I think most people there joined AMCU. I think out of a 100 per cent of people in Karee, 60 per cent joined AMCU and it was apparent that AMCU was the one ruling in Karee and it was a union for the workers.

INTERVIEWER: On what you just explained to me, can I please take you back a bit? You said when you started here you were a part of NUM?

MINEWORKER: NUM, truly speaking, it always sides with the employer and not the workers that is what NUM does and I will

---

2   This is contested by the NUM. See Chapter 2 note 6.

not hide that because someone dies underground, NUM and the employer agree that they should hide that person and we as workers we will try and find out what happened to that person and how did he get hurt here in the mine. When a person gets hurt here underground the employer and NUM change the story, they say that person got hurt in his shack, you see? Or they will say he got hurt wherever he stays but that person got hurt today and he got hurt underground and we have been trying to fight that thing here and we do not have power because the union is not showing us the way, so now we do not have power now to take over or take any further steps about that matter.

... What I can say my brother about NUM is that they are highly coincident, they don't want to talk to us about issues that they see that they are under pressure [about], they don't want to talk to us you see, they tell themselves that they are the only ones who have rights to go talk with the employer and they are the only ones that can take our grievances to the employer, but otherwise they cannot talk with us, and when we want a meeting with them, they don't want to organise a meeting with us so that we will be able to talk about our issues, that is NUM my brother.

INTERVIEWER: So you said that you had a strike? When they fired your chairperson?

MINEWORKER: We always voted for him because we loved our chairperson [Steve] and he worked the way we liked him to, even if they did not like him. The people from NUM never liked him because he always came with straight things to us. Our chairperson [told us] things that NUM never wanted us to know, like maybe things that management was saying to them. Our chairperson will tell us that 'men there is something that is going to happen and it is going to kill you'. He would tell us, but they did not want him to tell us those things... In the mine, when they hire you, they say you that you will work 8 hours 45 minutes a day, but we work 15 hours, 14 hours, 12 hours, because you are doing a job for three people alone. And you have to finish the work on the same day before you can go out. If you start work at 6 then you will go out at 7 at night. I work at night. I start work at 9 at night, but I only come out around 7, 8, until people who work day shift start work.

INTERVIEWER: What made your chairperson to be different?

MINEWORKER: He did not want to take bribery, because the mine deals with bribery. It bribes these people. They bribe our leaders to sign rules that will oppress workers. So he did not want that thing. He did not want to take bribery from management. He did not want that.

INTERVIEWER: When did you decide that you are going to strike?

MINEWORKER: We came out on that day, and it was on Tuesday [17 May 2011], and then we started the strike on Thursday, but I don't remember the date because it was last year. We started the strike on Thursday, and then it was Friday, and then Saturday, and we rested on Sunday. And then we resumed again on Monday… and then on Thursday [26 May] that is when they came… the people from the region. And they went to our employer and told them that they should fire us and then he did fire us… But what we wanted at that time was for them to tell us why they suspended our chairperson, and instead they went to our employer and told him to fire us because we don't want to work… Our employer fired us then, and he did re-employment and some people were never re-employed, even now…

INTERVIEWER: So in that three months [after the strike and before AMCU recruited] did you have meetings, or what were you doing?

MINEWORKER: In that three months the situation was bad, it was very bad because if you do not have a union the employer can do whatever he likes to you. We worked in rough conditions and we did not have rights to talk about our things you see, and yes we did organise meetings as workers, we organised meetings so that as workers we will sit and see how we can get a union, or maybe how do we get back to NUM you see… In fact the point was that how do we get a union you see, and at that time it was apparent that it would be hard because a majority of us did not want to get back to NUM, and we saw that we will welcome any other union at that time, whichever came at that time, and that is when AMCU came…

INTERVIEWER: So the decision that on the 9th you are meeting, how did that come about?

MINEWORKER: You see sir, as I have said, that Karee came here at Wonderkop [Stadium], and they meet people here, and they negotiated that, it was that day on the 9th, it was a holiday... That is when we meet here in Wonderkop and then they came here in Karee, then when they got here in Wonderkop, those from Eastern came here at Wonderkop. Then when they meet that is when they decided that on Friday 10 August they will go to the employer, and then they went... So okay after they made the decision that they will go to the employer on the 10th. Then on Friday [10 August] they meet, all the RDOs. But at that time we [non-RDOs] were still at work, but we were not working because there will be no job without the RDOs there. And then the RDOs went to the offices of the employer...

On the same day the employer went to his office and called NUM, our leaders... The NUM responded to the employer by saying that the employer should tell us that we have no right to go to the employer, and we should have talked with them first before they went to the employer. And then the employer came back to us and told us that NUM had called him and they told me that you have no right to go to the employer, as we have not told them, which means you went behind his back. And the workers did not fight. They just came back to the stadium on Friday on the same day... Then on Saturday they came here [the stadium] and they had talks here in the morning, and that time, when they ended the report, they said now no one will be going to work on Saturday night shift.

INTERVIEWER: So you all meet on Saturday morning [11 August]?

MINEWORKER: Yes, we meet on Saturday in the morning and then on Saturday morning that is when we all meet because I was there also there doing everyone's job now because they were not choosing anymore now, who did what and who did that. And then on that day we meet and we said we were going to the NUM offices here in Wonderkop because in Karee they have no offices there. And then we went to their offices but when we were near the offices we found them outside, those people, our leaders, I can put it like that, they came out. Our leaders came out of the offices already having guns and, they just came out shooting...

INTERVIEWER: So when you look, why do you think the union that you are paying is not protecting you and shooting at you?

MINEWORKER: What they don't want is us getting money and I am very sure of that, they don't want us to get money. When we went to them and told them, no man go to the employer and tell them that we want 12.5 they knew we will never get it because they are the ones who are always standing with management.

INTERVIEWER: When you went to NUM while marching there did you have your weapons then?

MINEWORKER: No, we did not have weapons on that day... we got our weapons in the veld and we sat and talked about that. Now we are sleeping in the veld and we are not sleeping in our houses anymore because we were [afraid] that NUM people will come to our houses door to door to shoot us, you see? So we decided that it was better that we stay there in the veld and that is when we slept there and we would share money to buy bread and cold drinks and make a fire. Yes and we talked about safety there and we decided to get our weapons now and we stayed in the veld because we felt safe when we had them.

INTERVIEWER: So when you go get your weapons because you are staying in the mountain who were you afraid will attack you?

MINEWORKER: NUM... we were afraid of NUM that they will attack us.

INTERVIEWER: So it was NUM that pushed you into carrying weapons?

MINEWORKER: Yes, because they shot at us and we were afraid then that they will come back, and we do not have guns and so we thought it will be better that we have our traditional weapons.

INTERVIEWER: What happened on the 12th?

MINEWORKER: On the 12th we stayed there on that day, the whole day in the mountain, we were singing, talking and sharing ideas and encouraging each other that here is not the same as your house and one has to be strong and obviously people there in the mountain, and there are houses there and you are just sitting there, and making fire and we put money together and we don't even do the washing. We are just sitting there and doing nothing and waiting for the employer to come and because we do not even go to our houses because we are afraid that they will come and shoot us...

On the 13th... on Monday we found out that [there] are workers who were working at Karee and then we decided that we are going to choose people and I think we choose about plus minus thirty people from the Eastern camp to go and tell those people that we were in the veld and that is where we are staying and that they should come and join us. And at that time we already had our weapons and we did not walk through the township, we walked through the veld until we got to 3 Shaft and then we meet up with the mine police and they asked us where we were going and what we wanted and we told them that we were there to tell the people working in the shaft that we were at the mountain. That is where we are and they should come join us there and the mine police agreed and they told us that they will tell them and they went and told them and then we went back through the veld.

And while walking back in the veld, there is small place that we jump to and there is a little dam there and we were met by government police and I think they were going with maybe three Hippos and plus, minus, 20 vans. Not sure but they were many and they came and stopped us from the front and they said that we should give them our weapons and we said we will not be able to, not unless they escort us back to the mountain where the other workers are and there they will take all our weapons together. And the government police did not agree to that and what they did was that they said they will start to count to five and they started counting one, two, three, four, five and when he got to five they just started shooting and they shot one person dead and others were injured and we ran back to the mountain and we gave them the report that we meet up with the government police and they shot at us. And one is dead and others are injured and we did not all come back and then we explained what happened.

INTERVIEWER: And then on the 15th what happened?

MINEWORKER: They came again saying they wanted the five men and we gave them those five men to go talk with the police. And when they got to the police, then the police said they had brought the employer, and we said then he should talk with us, and when he spoke we heard that was no employer it was the president of NUM, Mr Zokwane. And Mr Zokwane said the only thing he came to tell us was that he wanted us to go back to work and that there was nothing else he was going to talk to us about, 'The only thing I am telling you is that you should all go back to work'. And we told him that he was not the employer of Lonmin, he was Zokwane and we asked how can he tell us to go back to work? And he said that he was going to tell us that we should go back to work, and that was the only thing he was going to talk to us about... we told him that we wanted the employer only there, and not him Zokwane. We said, 'We did not want you, we did not want AMCO, and we did not want NUM in our meetings. We only wanted the employer only', and then he left. Maybe after five minutes after he left, we saw another car coming and a Hippo, and in that car it was the AMCO president Mr Joseph Mathunjwa. And he said he had come by the government escort, and we said 'Then say what you have to say'... And then we said we do not want AMCO or NUM in our negotiations. The only thing we want is the employer, that's it... And then they left.

INTERVIEWER: And the 16th?

MINEWORKER: The government police came and they came with the same story again saying they wanted to build a relationship with us. And we told to them to do what they wanted but we wanted them to explain to us how they were going to build that relationship with us. And they said they were going to sit there with us to protect us because we were sitting on government property, and we said okay we can sit, and we sat there... but what amazed me the most is that this time when they came they came with razor wires in the back of their trailers, all the Hippos were pulling that wire and we wondered what were they going to do now and then they tried to put us inside that wire and we told them no we do not want any protection and we did not want them putting that thing around us and we said they should take it back wherever they took it from and they said okay and then we sat down and we sang our songs.

INTERVIEWER: So according to them were they only closing the whole place or were they just closing a small place?

MINEWORKER: On that side by the shack there that is where they were closing from, there where there are electricity poles, where there are smelters going down there, they were closing there going all the [way] down and they stopped here in the corner and that is when we asked them to stop putting us inside that razor wire, you see? Because we did not trust them too because we did not know if they were also going to beat us too or what... they left it there and then in the afternoon Mr Joseph Mathunjwa from AMCO came and he said that we should go back to our houses because he thinks we are not safe there anymore in the mountain and that we should meet the next morning because 'our employer was not willing to come there and meet you and because I went back today and I told him that you wanted to meet him and he is not willing to come here. And because this thing I don't trust it anymore, and I think you are not safe here anymore. I think your employer and NUM have planned something big and I think that it is better that you go home'. And we told him that we are not going to separate and we are not going anywhere because this place is like our homes now. We have been there eating there and making the fire there and we cannot even do our washing, we don't do washing, we have been eating bread every day there, we are not going anywhere, we are staying here.

And we sat and then he said, 'okay if you don't want to go then there is nothing I can do about that', and we [were] told to go. [We had said that] we told you before that we do not want any union here, which union, then we said we needed the employer there only and then he went to his car at that time and there was no escort. Then he came back on foot, and then we asked him where was the government escort then and he said management did not want to give him the escort so that he will be able to come to us. But [we responded to him] yesterday they said that all leaders should be escorted according to the government rules, so how come you don't have it now? And they said management did not give them the escort as AMCU and then we just came back on foot because we know that you are people and we will come to you and talk to you but you are telling us now that we should go and we are going.

And we said to them that they should go and tell this man, that management of Lonmin that we are only looking for the employer here and whatever the employer has planned is none of your business and that the only thing he can do is go and tell the employer that we want to talk to him and that, 'Sir, we want R12,500 and if you do not have it now then tell us when you will have it, and tell us what you have now and we will hold on to that and go back to work'.

Our employer did not agree to that too and we did not worry about that and then Mr Joseph Mathunjwa left at that time and then at around 12... no okay at around 3 in the afternoon, he came back and he said I am here to beg you as workers and he even went down on his knees and he was crying too here in front of us. He said, 'Please men go and you will meet again in the morning tomorrow, you should separate and everyone should go to their houses'. And then we told him that we are afraid of going to our houses because we did not know who was going to come and that we are staying there and it is better that whatever happens will happen if Lonmin, government has planned that.

Okay. He left now around 3, 4, and when it was 4 the police started again to join that razor wire and we asked them please do not close that razor wire, please. And they stopped, I think for about thirty minutes, but we sat there, and when it was five they came back again, and we saw two soldier Hippos coming and join them, and eight soldiers came out of the Hippos carrying guns and now there were many police there also carrying those big guns. I don't know what they call them, each and every police was carrying his own gun and they arranged a line, a line that was very long. I am sure it was about 100 metres because these policemen were many and while we were still looking at that we saw the mine bus approaching, those big joined buses from the mine. There were two buses, and when these buses were now near the other police it stopped, and a lot of police came to join them in that line, and now they [the line of police] were coming from Wonderkop to Marikana at the top there, from the veld there. And we were now surrounded by police, and they came one by one and they were all carrying those big guns. And while that was happening the two white Hippos came on reverse, and they came here, and there were two other soldier Hippos that joined them from the front. And the soldiers appeared on top of the Hippos with their guns. And the other Hippo now was pulling that razor wire, joining it to the other one near the shacks. And, maybe, when there was space, maybe it was 20 metres or 30 metres, I don't remember correctly, but we saw other soldiers and then another Hippo coming, the third one. But what really amazed me was that the truck that carries water and the other one that carries tear gas, they were nowhere near, they were standing right at the back, very far.

But I was now worried seeing that something was about to happen and we sat down and the police are not talking to us at this point, they are busy with their jobs now and while that was happening another soldier Hippo came but it was a bit smaller than the other ones and another one again and then another one again, now the third one and the police Hippo came, and then another one and then the third one and it came very near to us and when they came there was another white man there wearing a brown trouser and a white shirt, and he [was] big in his body and he was telling the other police to come near in the line, and the police, the soldiers in the Hippo started shooting at us then and they shot one person at that time, they hit him with a bullet here in his head, here in the back and it came out in front and while we were still listening to that then we started running and when we tried to run these Hippos were coming stronger at us and now the police had started shooting also now and the Hippos were coming at us and some were run over and I am sure many people were killed there by being ran over and some were shot with guns and now I get very amazed when the police say they were defending themselves. What were they defending themselves from? What had happened that made them defend themselves?

INTERVIEWER: So in your mind what do you think, how do you feel and what are you thinking?

MINEWORKER: Hey my man, my head was not working on that day and I was very, very numb and very, very nervous, because I was scared. I never knew of such things. I only knew of them like what had happened in 1976 and what happened in 1992, because of history. I would hear about massacres you see. I usually heard of that from history, but on that day it came back, so that I can see it. Even now, when I think back, I feel terrible, and when I reverse my thinking to that, I feel sad still.

INTERVIEWER: Now what are you thinking about the police?

MINEWORKER: The police? No, I don't like them, and even if he can step on my toe in a shop at Shoprite maybe I will slap him, because I don't want to see a police or even talk to them. I want nothing to do with them. I will just look at them. And they are like dogs to me now. And even if I have a police officer in the family, but they know that I don't get along with the police at all. When I see a police now I feel like throwing up.

INTERVIEWER: So if you see a crime will you report [it] to the police or...?

MINEWORKER: I will not, my brother. They will see that for themselves. Even if I was attacked I don't think I will go to them because I do not trust them anymore. They are like my enemies now.

Mineworker 9

INTERVIEWER: How are the living conditions in the mines?

MINEWORKER: Not good at all, eight people live in one room and share the dining room, it was a health hazard because if someone fell sick in front of you or they go to hospital and come back you run the risk of contracting the illness.

INTERVIEWER: What kind of job do you do?

MINEWORKER: I am an RDO, I grind the rock.

INTERVIEWER: How are the working conditions at the mine?

MINEWORKER: The working conditions are very poor. Number one, the working places are in bad conditions, number two, the hours are very long, if your eight hours pass and you haven't reached the day's target then your hours will exceed the eight hours. You have to blast every day and if you leave without doing this you will be held accountable... We drill the stone so that we can extract platinum in the rock, firstly drill the holes in the rock, then clean them, after that we put explosives so that platinum can be extracted, then we take it from the surface.

INTERVIEWER: Were you also part of the strike that demanded R12,500?

MINEWORKER: That is the truth which I cannot deny, like now we are not working we don't even know when we will go back to work, but we are pleading with the government to increase our salary; the money that we are getting right now is an insult. What we do not want is to lose our jobs, we want our money that is it. Now we are have to pay R200 rent everything which is deducted from my pay every month and how much am I left with in the R5,000 that I get every month? Look at my body this is not my original skin all that you are seeing right now is because of the platinum. It has bad effects on my skin and in a couple of years when I fall sick the company will abandon me, because R5,000 is nothing when your wife and children depend on you.

INTERVIEWER: How did this strike start?

MINEWORKER: Two weeks before the week of the 16th all the shafts gathered to discuss the poor working conditions we are subjected to and low income we receive, but because we were members of the NUM union led by Mr Zokwana which dismally failed to represent worker's needs. We have been misled by leaders all the time, we found out that our complaints were not even reaching the employer so we decide to approach the employer ourselves so that we could find out whether or not he would increase our pay. On the holiday of the 9th indeed we went there as workers and RDOs because our job is very difficult. As planned we went to Number 1 where our employer is based, we didn't receive any answers from them, when we got there we were approached by a white man who told us that our employer will address us in 15 minutes, he is aware of our request, only to find out he lied, because we waited and waited.

What was puzzling us was that he said the employer was aware of our request but how did he know it since we didn't approach him. We decide to go straight to our employer who didn't give us anything. On the same day of the 9th we went back to the stadium to discuss a way forward, we did not involve NUM on this, so we decided that the following day we would take a trip to NUM offices to admit our mistakes and try to figure out how we could get hold of our employer so that we could get straight answers, we went there on a Saturday.

Ten minutes before we got to the union offices we were met by NUM comrades. That is where they started shooting at us, that is where two of our comrades lost their life, it become clear that we were not accepted by the very union we voted for, and it also showed that they had strong relationships with our employers. We run to the mountain where we all gathered... in the mountain, when we got here we realised that we didn't have anywhere else to run to, the union was killing us and the employer didn't want to address us, so we decided to get out of the mine property, go and stay in the mountain instead, land was owned by the government who we voted for, so we thought this would be the only place where we could take refuge.

We slept there because we were afraid to go back to our homes, we slept there on Sunday and when we woke up we discussed a way forward since our employer wanted nothing to do with us, so we had to find a way to get through to the union then use that to get to the employer. That is where mine securities denied us access... so that we explained to them that we were not fighting we just wanted to speak to our employer and hand over the list of our demands. All we wanted was a way to meet with the employer, we went there by force that is where we decided to stand up for ourselves, they started shooting at us, we fought back till they run and we went back to the mountain. On Monday the police came and said they wanted to build peace and since we didn't have anyone on our side, we asked their names.

They said no they couldn't do that, so we asked them to bring the employer back. They left and came back on Tuesday to discuss demands. We told them that we would not leave the mountain until we spoke to our employer and our demands were met. Because they wouldn't communicate the way we wanted to communicate with our employer.

The police left and came back on the 16th. By this time they were very angry, they came with comrade Zokwana in a Hippo. We have a combination of all African languages, Zulu, Sotho, Shangaan and Xhosa here in the mines called Fanakalo. He said, 'My fellow comrades it is not that I fought with you.' His statement was made by one of the police, 'I came here to build peace.'

INTERVIEWER: What exactly did he say?

MINEWORKER: He said, 'My brothers I am back, yesterday I went back to get answers and your employer made it clear that he had nothing to say to you.' He said he was a visitor so he wanted to speak to us in the Hippo because he was scared.

INTERVIEWER: Scared of Zokwana you mean?

MINEWORKER: He was scared of Zokwana, we told him we will not harm your visitor, all we wanted [was] to see the face of the visitor. He said he didn't feel safe, we told him all we wanted was to talk to our employer. He said we must elect five people to go and speak to him, we agreed on this so that we could hear what he had said, unfortunately three of those were killed on that day, we released the man as requested, they instructed us to leave behind all our weapons, it was already past 6 we told them when they got to the Hippo to tell him to come back on Thursday, comrade Zokwana said that is not what he come there to do, he said he come to instruct us to go back to work, we said we were not going to argue with you. We instructed him to address the crowd as requested. He took the speaker and said tomorrow you must all return to work, we responded by saying we will not go back to work not until we were addressed by our employer, he then left and said he was going to fetch the background, whatever that means.

We released five more men to go and ask police in the Hippo that we wanted to sleep, if they wanted to speak to us they must return tomorrow morning at 9am, indeed they left and we slept on the 15th. We didn't have anything to eat whilst staying in the mountain, we were helped by the people in the nearby shacks who brought us food, we were scared to go back to our own homes, fear of being killed. On the morning of the 16th we saw soldiers who came from Marikana approaching us, it was at around 8am we shouted for the other workers, it was one car, there was a cloth covering a machine that was pointing at us, we requested all the other comrades to come down from the top, while still dealing with that five Hippos were also arriving with the razor fence, again we sent five more men to go tell them not to put up the fence, they went there and asked them not to fence the area until we spoke to the employer. They said we had nothing to do with mines we were sent here by government to come and do a job. We asked them what we did wrong because we didn't harm anyone, we asked them whether it would [be] possible for some of them to go with the five comrades to speak to their employer so that we could ask him who did we harm by staying on the mountain.

INTERVIEWER: Did they say who sent them?

MINEWORKER: They said their boss sent them there, they did mention the name of that person, just can't remember it, but some comrades know the name of the person. The AMCO president also promised us yesterday that he would return today to give us a report back, when he arrived with his people he was kicked out and they didn't allow him to come in, Zokwana and his people were taking over, he told us that he had tried to speak to our employer as previously agreed upon but to no avail, word also come out that we were going to be killed on that day. The AMCO comrade came back in the afternoon at round about 2, he warned us to leave the mountain because our employer and the government made an agreement to come and kill us.

NUM said it did not have any members in the mountain, all those members there belonged to AMCO. As AMCO president I come to plead with you to leave the mountain and go back to work, we will try and fix this later on, we said comrade go back home you did your best, but we will not leave here till we got the R12,500 pay we are requesting, and if we had to die fighting for that so be it. Madiba fought for this country and he made it clear that violence does not solve anything, we should talk and negotiate through striking that is how Mandela fought for our country. He left and it was already past 3 by then, he come back then again and asked to pray for us as it was time, as he left, they started putting up the fence till to a place next to a kraal, they threw something that looked like a bird which was controlled through a remote control, the soldiers that had come in the morning came back in their car and another police Hippo also arrived, one man come out of the car and shouted fire and they started shooting.

INTERVIEWER: You mentioned you lived here on the mountain, also that there was a place where a lot of people were slaughtered, [the] fence was put up and shacks on the other side. What exactly did you see in the scene?

MINEWORKER: Let me start with the mountain, as you can see the mountain is high [and] we chose it deliberately after NUM killed our members and so that we could easily see people when they come, we could see Marikana and the other place near us, the bush nearby is where most people were arrested after they started splashing us with water and the green water, people run to the mountain and that is where they were caught, they were surrounded by police.

INTERVIEWER: What about this area where they said they found blood and people's clothes. Did people also die there?

MINEWORKER: A lot of people died there, that is where some of our members went in and never came back... the people who ran into the bush were the ones being transported [in ambulances and police trucks].

INTERVIEWER: Thank you very much for your time.

Mineworker 10

INTERVIEWER: What do you do when you are not working on weekends?

MINEWORKER: I do my washing, after that I go to church at past three, because at ZCC they have church services every single day at three. I also love soccer so sometimes I go to the gym to train, I alternate—if I do not go to church today I will go tomorrow. Also if I go to gym today then tomorrow I will go to church just like that because I love the gym.

INTERVIEWER: How would you describe the working conditions here at the mines?

MINEWORKER: The working conditions here are very bad, I didn't even think that I will last five years working here, but because I have no choice, I need the money I have to work. But the conditions we worked under are not right at all... First the places we live in are not right, the pay is not right, the workplace is also not right, the salary we're getting is an insult compared to the hard job we do every single day, we weren't even supposed to be getting R4,000 but because we having nothing else on the hand we have to work otherwise we would not even be here.

INTERVIEWER: What is NUM's view on this situation?

MINEWORKER: When I was employed here in 2006 I was under NUM but since then nothing has changed, the same poor working conditions that my father was subjected to, I am also working under those conditions. As you can see we live in shacks, when we arrive here we lived in hostels but as soon as you get a housing allowance you move out to the shacks, everything is hot here, the mine is hot and everything in the mine shaft is closed; sometimes we do not even get air or water so dust is the only thing we get, we use a cage to go under and the rope that holds the cage can tear any time. The NUM union exists but there is nothing that it has ever succeeded in addressing any of the workers' issues that have occurred, it goes to speak to the employers but never reports anything concrete to the workers, so it is useless. It has not done anything for me as a worker, it is not as if I have a complaint it will be addressed. All it ever says is that the boss said this and this, but it has never succeeding in addressing any problem.

INTERVIEWER: So now this strike, how did it start? What was the issue that fuelled the strike?

MINEWORKER: With regards to the strike what happened is that workers met at Wonderkop Stadium on the 9th with [the] aim to discuss wage increase as workers. Upon discussion on the 9th we decided to involve all the mines at Lonmin and we all agreed that we were not getting paid accordingly. When we met on the 9th we all agreed that the workers should go to the employer and represent themselves, not the unions, because they are the very unions who never come back with anything logical, all they ever say is feedback, feedback all year long but they never report anything rational to the workers. We as workers decided to approach our employer face to face so that we can directly give him a list of our demands and get a direct response from him.

We decided to do this ourselves instead of always relying on the union who never gives us any form of report so we decided to do this ourselves this time around, we were tired of not getting any answers. Maybe the so-called union didn't even approach the employer, they [are] just fooling us. We wanted to inform him of the problems we were experiencing and how we can address them and meet us half way so we can move forward. So we all agreed that the RDO will represent us because they are responsible for ensuring that work gets done, maybe with them representing us we might receive rational feedback, also that some of the workers must go back to work so that we do not all abandon work. So on Friday all the RDOs went to the employer, and some of the workers went to work. RDOs met at Wonderkop and went to Number 1 to approach the employer.

On their way to the employer they were blocked by the securities, because usually when we approach the employer we sing songs, upon their arrival there they were stopped by the security guards, the workers approached the guards, we came peacefully, all we want is to see our employer. That was not a problem, the securities opened for them. When they arrived there they met someone who claimed to be our employer, he asked what do you want here, we said we want our employer. He said that your union NUM said that it did not have any members here in this mine, so you have no right to be here, your union needs to be the one approaching me. The truth is we did not inform any union—we wanted to approach the employer by ourselves so that we can get a direct response. He was right, it turned out that we needed to inform NUM and tell them that we did not want it to represent us, we wanted to represent ourselves. We made a mistake on not informing the union that we took a decision to approach our employer by ourselves, nonetheless we went back on Friday. It was then decided that on Saturday we will go back to the workers and inform them what happened and what went wrong. Indeed we acknowledged that we made a mistake that even though we did not want them to represent us, we should have at least informed them...

We united and went as previously agreed, and on Friday we decided that all the workers should boycott work on Saturday so that we could go and inform NUM of our intentions and after that go straight to the employer. On Saturday, I think it was the 11th, as agreed upon workers gathered at the stadium on Saturday, the RDO informed the workers of their journey, so we walked to the NUM offices to inform [them] that yesterday we decided to take such action but we were blocked because we did not inform you as our leaders so the aim of this visit is to inform you of our actions because there are certain things which we want to hear directly from the employer, on top of that you have not given us any satisfactory feedback, so we want to know from the employer what [it] is that was not clear with our complaints which were directed to him.

Halfway through the NUM offices we were singing and no one was holding any weapon. When the NUM saw us approaching its offices it didn't even ask, it just opened bullets on the workers. Everyone ran for cover. No one expected this to happen, we thought as its members it would welcome us and hear what we had to say and criticise us because it had the right to criticise us after we went over its head so that we could apologise for going over its head because we were supposed to inform it first before we went there. Instead of doing that they fired bullets at us and two RDOs were killed instantly, the rest of us ran to the stadium. When we got there securities closed the stadium, we could not go in, so we ran to our respective areas where [we] lived. On the following day we met... Upon arrival the securities had closed the stadium, on top of that I wasn't even there on Sunday. I heard it from people that a security van was burned and two security guards where dead.

... [On Tuesday] they said, 'workers we are not fighting with you, we come in peace we are pleading with you to go back to your job and resolve your issues.' We have never heard the police speak in Fanakalo before but that day they did. We didn't care much about who was making the announcement. We were just at peace that who-ever was making the announcement was in a police Hippo that is all we cared about. They requested [the] top five [madoda] to come and speak with them. As requested the people went there and it turned out there was some misunderstanding between the various speakers. The people were refused entry into the Hippo. The person who was speaking in the Hippo used a speaker. We told them, 'We were not going back to work till we spoke to the employer.' That day passed, then on Wednesday a man by the name of Zokwana, leader in the NUM, arrived in a Hippo. We didn't see him. We were just informed to listen to our leader. He was supposed to get off the Hippo, come down and address the people. The top five that was requested told him, 'We appreciate you coming here but we want you to address the people on the ground.' That was on Thursday. He said he had noth-ing to say to us, all we need to do is to go back to work. We asked him again to come and address the people on the ground, he could even be escorted by the soldiers or the police if he wanted to. And he said he is going to call AMCU.

Indeed we saw [an] AMCU van heading our way with Zokwana. They said, 'Workers, we wanted to approach you peacefully because we know that you are human, you are not animals. So we come to speak with you.' But we told them that the law does not allow us to come and speak with them directly, 'We will stand where [we] would rather stay, on the mountain.' Although they arrived in Hippos we could recognise their voices. When they arrived, Mr Zokwana did not say anything. AMCU said that the employer wants to come and speak to us, but because it was late he could not come and the situation was not looking very good. We said it was okay, we wanted to see the employer tomorrow at 9.

INTERVIEWER: Who said that you were going to meet with the employer at 9? Was it perhaps AMCU?

MINEWORKER: It was us the workers because we were informed that the employer wanted to come and see us but because it was late, I think it was around 6... we suggested that he comes tomorrow at 9. When we arrived on Thursday we were hopeful that our employer was coming at 9 to listen to our issues and hopefully address them all. But this did not happen. 9 passed [and] instead the place became flooded by police. AMCU arrived on Thursday the 16th in the afternoon but this time they were not escorted, without the Hippo. We asked them, 'What happened to the Hippo?' They said they went to the police and asked them to be escorted. The police said no they must go without the Hippo. It became clear that only important people like Zokwana were escorted. They told us that they set up a meeting to meet with the employer in the morning, but he never pitched. We asked where he was. They said he went to some meeting somewhere. We asked where the other unions were. They said that was none of our business. We tried calling our employer to find out where he was and again— we were told that has nothing to do with us.

They said as AMCU, they advise us to go back to work because if we stay there any longer, [a] lot of people might die, because they did not have the power to protect us. We told them we agreed the situation was looking bleak and we appreciate everything they have done for us but now they had to leave, we do not need any union to start with. And this had nothing to do with both AMCU and NUM who shot at us, because even Zokwana himself addressed us in a Hippo and didn't say anything rational to us anyways. About 20 minutes after they left we saw [more] Hippo, the other ones had soldiers and the other police. The first three Hippos passed us. It was carrying soldiers and they were followed by police. But we were not bothered by this at all because we did not wrong anyone. We were just waiting for the employer to come and address this issue. When the Hippos drew closer they started putting a razor wire so to trap us inside.

INTERVIEWER: What time did this happen?

MINEWORKER: It was late in the afternoon around five or [somthing] to five, we saw the razor wire and the Hippos were also drawing closer and closer. We saw that, no, things were bad and we had no one to turn to because we had no lawyers, nothing. Our only hope was that we did nothing wrong but everyone dispersed. One man went to the Hippo and pleaded with them that we, did not understand why they brought the razor wire. [We explained that they were the ones who] removed us from the ground where we used to meet and that we were also human. We come here but we [were] also disturbed, where else must we go. They just ignored him and continued fencing the area. We tried to find an opening where we could escape; as we were about to get out a Hippo stood in front of us so we were trapped...

Near the kraal that is where we tried to escape. The police used the Hippo to block the way while some were inside the Hippo and others outside behind it with guns pointing at people. If anyone tried to escape they were shot at. The first gun went off and the rest followed. There was a white policeman who said, 'fire'. It become chaos, people were stamped by the Hippo, water and teargas were used after the bullets which was pointless because whoever choked on the teargas was stamped by the Hippo. Most people who died were stamped by the Hippos. They used teargas to make them dizzy, then stamped on them. They lied about rubber bullets, they did not use them. There were also helicopters that were shooting at my fellow brothers. Some people were just passing by and had nothing to do with this [but nevertheless] died. Some brought food to their brothers and got caught in the crossfire and died. As you can see we are still living under the same conditions, we are not [even] eating anything.

INTERVIEWER: When you look at what happened do you think the workers will cancel their memberships with them?

MINEWORKER: I am most definitely sure that they will cancel their memberships, because everyone blames the NUM for the loss of their loved ones, some are in wheelchairs. If NUM had waited for our mandate none of this would have happened. So I want to say we blame the employer for not caring about us because as a parent, as a head of office, if there is dispute in the family he will go and address it, find out what is the problem so that his children will lay their hearts on the table, tell him these are our problems and this is how we want it to be resolved so that we can get this and this. He will ask for a chance and say I still have one, two, three to resolve so [he] will also address your problem. If he had done this the two people would still be alive and not followed by 34 deaths. NUM shot its own people. He was supposed to come while we were still staying in the mountain to come and address these issues.

6

Analysis and conclusion

Peter Alexander

The Marikana Massacre seized the lives of at least 34 people, nearly all of them striking workers employed by Lonmin. It was an exceptional event, at least for South Africa. In 1992 the Ciskei Defence Force killed 28 anti-apartheid activists in Bhisho. In the same year about 40 people died at Boipatong, but in that case the Inkatha Freedom Party, rather than the state, was the main culprit.[1] One has to go back to the Soweto Uprising of 1976 to find an example of government security forces murdering more protesters than at Marikana.[2] The last time such a large number of *strikers* was killed was in 1922, but most of those deaths occurred in an event known as a 'revolt', rather than a massacre, and soldiers, as well as workers, lost their lives.[3] There were considerably fewer fatalities during celebrated strikes by black mineworkers that occurred in 1920, 1946 and 1987. What is especially galling is that the atrocity occurred, not under an apartheid regime hostile to the black majority, but under a democratically elected government. Around the world, the victory of 1994 was greeted with excitement and high hopes, but the champion of the oppressed, the African National Congress (ANC), has now been revealed as the oppressor.

A seismic event, Marikana produced new faults from existing tectonic stress. Our account has examined the quake from the viewpoint of the workers; 'from the mountain' as it were. It is necessarily provisional, and the Commission of Inquiry, chaired by Judge Farlam, will yield further data. Yet it provides a perspective that is vital for balanced assessments, not only because it comes from the side of the slain, but also as an antidote to the dominant storyline. Jane Duncan conducted an analysis of sources used in South African newspapers in their coverage of Marikana and Lonmin from 12 to 22 August, a moment when opinions were strongly influenced. This shows that 27 per cent of references were business sources, 14 per cent were managers and owners of mines, and only three per cent were 'workers'.[4] This bias was shaped, supplemented and re-enforced by dramatic footage of the killings taken by TV cameras conveniently located just behind the police front-line.[5] With honourable exceptions, journalists lacked the credibility, commitment and patience to build the trust necessary to get the workers' story. Our own revelations about the Killing Koppie were first published on 21 August, but it was a further ten days before knowledge of these events seeped into mainstream media, and by then the police's version of what happened was firmly entrenched.[6] In concluding this book, we draw on our alternative narrative and other available sources to assess culpability for this tragic event and to offer pointers towards an analysis of pre-existing stress and post-facto faults.

More smoke than light

Two presumptions, each providing more smoke than light, prevailed in early media accounts. The first theory, advanced by Lonmin, the South African Police Service (SAPS) and Susan Shabangu, the Minister of Mineral Resources, was that violence was all about rivalry between the National Union of Mineworkers (NUM) and the Association of Mineworkers and Construction Union (AMCU).[7] While this was denied by NUM, its bellicose attacks on AMCU lent substance to the claim.[8] In visiting Marikana on 18 August, it was rapidly apparent that the strike united the workforce and cut across unions. Later there were reports that 11 of the workers who died in the massacre were NUM members, with 17 coming from AMCU. Marikana represented a rank and file rebellion, not an inter-union dispute, and this comes out clearly in our interviews. On other mines where there were similar revolts against the owners and NUM, there were no AMCU members. One does not want to belittle the role of AMCU activists at Marikana who campaigned for a living wage and won the support of fellow workers for a famous strike, but the union was more a consequence than a cause of trouble at the mine.

The second theory was that strikers charged at the police because they were 'high' on *muti* provided by a *sangoma* (that is, they had received a natural remedy from a traditional healer capable of communicating with ancestral spirits). This explanation was first propounded by a senior officer who had viewed the mountain from a police helicopter.[9] My first response when reading the story was one of ridicule, since miners taking muti is hardly newsworthy. Mining is dangerous and some mineworkers use muti on the grounds that it might reduce the chance of death or injury (in this respect it is similar to praying). Sitting on a mountain surrounded by armed police—including helicopters above—is also dangerous, and taking muti is a rational response, as it has been in other strikes.[10] However, in our interviews and numerous conversations there was no suggestion that muti was actually a source of courage, unlike singing and traditional weapons. In practice, the sangoma story was part of a discourse depicting the strikers as frenzied savages.[11] Emphasis on the sangoma, rather than the muti, resonates with the old 'agitator theory' of strikes, which is now widely discredited (partly because it is normative rather than explanatory, and partly because it assumes workers are merely ciphers).[12]

Culpable 1: Police and government

In assessing the massacre we should foreground the reality that, very probably, the 34 people who died on 16 August were all killed by the police. In the famous televised incident, police opened fire on a contingent of workers using R5 assault rifles, and within ten seconds 12 of them were fatally wounded. Over the next hour, perhaps less, a further 21 or 22 workers were slaughtered. The police defended its use of 'maximum' or 'lethal' force on three grounds. First, action had to be taken to end an illegal gathering that was a threat to public safety.[13] Second, as Riah Phiyega, Commissioner of the South African Police Service, the country's top cop, explained in a press conference held the day after the massacre, the intention was to 'disperse the protesters from their stronghold into smaller groups which would be more manageable for the police to disarm'.[14] Thirdly, the police fired in self-defence.[15]

On legality, it is worth noting that South Africa's Constitution provides for the right to strike and the right to freedom of assembly.[16] Strikes might be 'unprotected', meaning that employers can sack workers involved, but they cannot, on their own, be 'illegal' in the normal sense of 'in breach of the law'. Freedom of assembly is limited by the requirement that participants are 'unarmed'; however, traditional weapons are not necessarily 'arms' (they are, for instance, used in weddings, sport, farming and self-protection). In any case, it is difficult to see how men sitting on a mountain posed any immediate threat to the public. On the other hand, as the senior advocate George Bizos informed the Farlam Commission: 'Lethal force [as deployed by the police] is not sanctioned by our common law, by any legislation or by the Constitution'.[17]

In South Africa, 'dispersal' is a fairly common public order problem and the police handle it using rubber bullets, tear gas, water cannons, stun grenades and birdshot. When necessary, these can be fired from armoured vehicles and/or helicopters, thereby avoiding use of men on foot, who would be more vulnerable. However, General Phiyega wanted to *disarm* the strikers as well as *disperse* them. Given that sticks, spears and machetes are easily obtained, this objective had doubtful merit, but let us put that to one side. 'Disarming' could have been achieved with relatively few casualties had it been undertaken once workers reached their hostels, shacks and houses, and, in practice, this is what happened during the weeks following the massacre. The clear implication is that the police had a further motive. Why else would they mobilise special paramilitary units trained to use automatic weapons against armed cash-in-transit gangs?[18] It was these units that led the massacre. Why insist on sealing the gap in the fence when a narrow passage could have been deployed to disarm dispersing strikers? And, why make little or no use of rubber bullets and the regular public order arsenal until after a barrage of automatic gunfire?

The 'self-defence' argument is difficult for the police to sustain. As we have seen, the protesters were not attacking the police and none of

Marikana: A View from the Mountain and a Case to Answer

the police were injured. Photographs made available to the Inquiry reveal that weapons were placed beside the bodies of dead workers, implying that police had a need to fabricate evidence that supported their case.[19] Moreover, the police made no serious attempt to deter their 'attackers' by letting off rubber bullets or warning shots or, as a last resort, single R5 rounds rather than automatic fire. Further, the self-defence claim is belied by the merciless killing that occurred after the initial carnage. There was the use of Hippos to crush protesters' bodies, the events at the Killing Koppie and, as we now know from autopsy reports, 14 striking miners were shot from behind.[20] Others, including Mambush, had bodies that were riddled with bullets.

An alternative explanation is readily at hand. Just prior to the massacre, on the same day, Captain Dennis Adriao, spokesperson for SAPS in the North West Province (where Marikana is located), told the media: 'Today is unfortunately D-day'.[21] This formulation clearly conveyed the reality that Marikana was not about public order policing. The scale of mobilisation, the deployment of paramilitary units dressed in army fatigues and the use of R5 machine guns all strongly suggest that the police operation was planned like an act of warfare; part of a war against the enemy at home, a class enemy.[22] The strikers had to be punished and a signal given to unruly protesters elsewhere. Ronnie Kasrils, a former ANC Minister of Intelligence, captured the logic perfectly. There was, he said, 'an order from on high' to 'carry out a dangerous and dubious operation to clear an isolated, stony outcrop of desperate strikers armed with sticks and spears often referred to as "cultural" weapons in our country'. He concluded:

> These people were hardly occupying some strategic point, some vital highway, a key city square. They were not holding hostages. They were not even occupying mining property. Why risk such a manoeuvre other than to drive the strikers back to work at all costs on behalf of the bosses who were anxious to resume profit making operations?[23]

There is no need to speculate about the identity of the person who gave the 'order from on high'. Given that police were mobilised from different provinces around the country and that the use of 'maximum force' was contrary to police rules, the decision must have been taken at the very top of SAPS.[24] When General Phiyega was 'asked who gave the police the order to shoot', she responded: '"As commissioner, I gave police the responsibility to execute the task they needed to do."'[25] That is, she obliged senior officers to utilise lethal force if they thought this necessary. The Minister of Police, Nathi Mthethwa, would have authorised this strategy. He had earlier supported an internal memorandum issued on 20 December 2011 instructing that 'the use of rubber and shotguns must be stopped with immediate effect'.[26] A deviation from this policy must have been cleared by him.[27] The only significant issue is whether President Jacob Zuma participated in the decision. It would have been foolhardy for a line minister to take such a far-reaching decision without checking with the president, and Zuma has not distanced himself from Mthethwa's judgment, so there is a high chance that he had prior knowledge of what would happen. At the very least, the inquiry must now press this issue. The political significance of Mthethwa's role is that the governing party, the ANC, is implicated in the massacre.

Culpable 2: Lonmin

The police worked closely with Lonmin, and the company is also worthy of blame. In 1973 this British-based firm, then called Lonrho, was described by Edward Heath, the Conservative prime minister, as 'an unacceptable face of capitalism', and many will feel this portrayal remains apt today. For instance, Lonmin's workers and people around its mines live in appalling conditions.[28] Moreover, despite claims that demands for increased pay were excessive, in 2011 Lonmin's CEO, Ian Farmer, earned 325 times as much as the average worker in the mining industry.[29] Eventually, of course, the company agreed to very substantial pay rises, with RDOs and others getting an extra 22 per cent, but that was *after* the massacre of its employees! One simple deed would have prevented this bloodbath. As elucidated by Bishop Jo Seoka, who attempted to broker talks on 16 August and was pivotal in facilitating the final settlement: 'The massacre could have been avoided if Lonmin's management had listened to the workers' concerns'.[30] Instead, the company preferred to mislead the public.

Workers assemble on, and in front of, the mountain (to the left) and the hillock (to the right). The photograph was taken on 16 August 2012, just before the president of AMCU had left.

On 13 August Lonmin boss Bernard Mokwena told the press he did not know what sparked the Marikana violence because he had not received any grievance, yet three days earlier workers had presented their complaints *en masse* (see narrative).[31] On 16 August Mokwena justified Lonmin's stance by claiming that it was 'illegal' to negotiate with the strikers.[32] Leaving his spurious claim about legality to one side, the issue here was one of 'listening', something that Lonmin had done several days earlier when awarding the RDOs a bonus, and something they would do again when the settlement was reached. In the meantime, others at Lonmin had been busy providing the police with valuable logistical support—barracks, transport, a detention camp and probably much more.

Culpable 3: National Union of Mineworkers

For socialists like me, who have been supporters of NUM for decades, it has been especially depressing to see the way the union's leadership has responded to the Marikana crisis. On 11 August, as we saw in Chapter 2, some NUM officials may have shot at unarmed strikers, two of whom were seriously wounded. Workers, genuinely believing that two of their comrades had been killed, headed for the mountain and gathered traditional weapons. This fed into the tragic events that culminated in the massacre. On 13 August Frans Baleni, NUM's general secretary, said: 'We appeal for the deployment of the Special Task Force or the South African Defence Force as a matter of urgency before things get out of hand'.[33] Whilst Baleni cannot be blamed for 34 deaths, one wonders whether the government adopted its stance after hearing his appeal. Baleni's immediate response to the massacre was to comment that 'all parties involved must take responsibility', but he quickly adjusted, adopting a defensive, hard-line stance.[34] In an opinion piece in the *Sunday Independent*, he blamed the employers, AMCU and strikers for the violence, but not the police. This lack of criticism was despite the fact that at least ten NUM members had been killed by the police (see appendix).[35]

How did this state of affairs come about? In his *Political Report* to this year's Congress of South African Trade Unions (COSATU) conference, held in mid-September, Zwelinzima Vavi, the federation's general secretary, bemoaned 'a growing distance between leaders and members, and a growth in negative perceptions amongst members about "corruption" in the movement'.[36] In terms of remuneration, this distance is nowhere greater than in NUM, where the general secretary is now paid R77,000 per month.[37] A gap also exists at a workplace level, where it is particularly insidious. According to former trade unionist Gavin Hartford:

> Earnings are a key issue. Once workers become shop stewards they are graded to C1 level and typically earn three times as much as the average worker. They are removed from production or underground work. They work in air-conditioned offices and have largely unrestricted movement across the operations. They get a range of perks and benefits, including significant time off for external union duties.[38]

Becoming a shaft steward can be the first rung in developing a new career, either within the company or in NUM. Union positions can lead to power and fame. Indeed, Cyril Ramaphosa, Kgalema Motlanthe (now Deputy President) and Gwede Mantashe all moved from holding the position of general secretary of NUM to being Secretary General of the ANC.[39] It would be wrong to simply equate advancement and opportunism. Union activists are often bright, committed and ambitious, and their own ability can take them into skilled, supervisory and management positions. The net effect, though, is to increase the separation between the union and members.[40] Promotion may also be a reason for the failure of NUM to improve the position of work organisation at the shaft level, leaving space for independent initiatives by workers.[41] Sociologists Sakhela Buhlungu and Andries Bezuidenhout list further factors producing weak shop steward organisation, including: 'internal conflicts, careerism, corruption, succession battles and tribalism or ethnicity'.[42]

Corruption is a recurring theme. The Congress of South African Trade Union's (COSATU's) *Workers Survey* showed that 20 per cent of NUM members in the survey had 'personally seen corruption' in their union, the highest figure for any union, and 43 per cent claimed that it existed.[43] As early as 2007 Bezuidenhout and Buhlungu pointed out that at Karee mine there were reports of jobs being sold, with one worker claiming that 'the price of a job was R1,500, half of which went to the shaft steward and the other half to the person in the human resources department of the company'.[44] Given that Karee was at the centre of the Marikana strike, this was a significant finding, and the company and NUM were surely aware of the problem, which, according to one of our interviewees, continued to exist. In an interview on the causes of the strike, Crispin Chinguno, a PhD student working on the platinum industry, responded to a question about why strikes were occurring now by stating bluntly: 'I think they [miners] have now realised NUM... is no longer on their side.' This assessment is vindicated by mass resignations from NUM at all three of the major platinum producers: Impala, Lonmin, and, now, the largest of them all, Angloplats.

COSATU has unequivocally backed NUM, its largest affiliate. An eight-page COSATU declaration on Marikana speaks of a 'tragedy' and never 'a massacre', and although it condemns 'the killings of 16th August' it fails to mention that the police were responsible. It complains that 'the Platinum bosses... have systematically undermined collective bargaining', but avoids reference to Marikana (the subject of the declaration), where the 'tragedy' flowed from Lonmin's defence of its collective bargaining agreement with NUM. There is a claim that the police are 'advancing the narrow interests of the employers', but this is described merely as a '*perception*'. SAPS, we are told, 'has consistently failed to *act*' in response to 'physical attacks against NUM members', but at Marikana they did *act*, doing so in line with NUM's call for action, and they killed ten or 11 of its members. This is ignored.[45] In the *Political Report*, Vavi follows his lambasting of 'distance' and 'corruption' with the statement that COSATU needs to avoid 'denialism about the extent of the challenges, or shirking responsibility for our role in addressing them'. It is difficult to avoid the conclusion that COSATU's response to Marikana was marked by 'denialism' and 'shirking'.[46] The approach adopted by the South African Communist Party (SACP), ally of the ANC and COSATU, took matters one step further. In his speech to the COSATU congress, SACP general secretary Blade Nzimande pledged his party's support for the 'government's crackdown', adding that 'the ring-leaders must be dealt with and separated from the mass of misled strikers.'[47] NUM's leaders are also part of the SACP leadership, and the party is closely identified with the Zuma faction in the ANC.

A triangle of torment and the labour relations regime

There is what one might call a *triangle of torment* linking Lonmin, the police and NUM. This extends beyond Marikana to include the government/ANC, big business (especially mining capital) and COSATU. Even the investment firm J.P. Morgan had spotted the problem, specifying: 'NUM has become too close to both mines' management and the ruling ANC... losing touch with its constituency.'[48] Hartford, a union sympathiser, speaks of a 'co-dependent comfort zone' inhabited by the union and mine owners.[49] Commenting on industrial conflict in his company, a Goldfields' spokesperson told radio listeners: 'Last time, NUM came to our assistance and we hope they will do so now.'[50] At the COSATU congress, Vavi denounced capitalists and then welcomed Patrice Motsepe, who had funded the event.[51] Motsepe, who is chair of Harmony Gold and has major interests in Anglo Platinum, is brother of Bridgette, who is married to Jeff

Women from Marikana convey the following opinion on 18 August 2012: 'Zuma, when are you taking over the mines? These ones have failed.'

Radebe, Minister of Justice.[52] Big business does not just rely on black partners, like Motsepe, to influence government; it frequently does it through threats to disinvest, actual disinvestment, and sometimes refusal to invest. These are strikes by another name. Relationships within the triangle are, however, not always cosy and there are sometimes tensions—such as COSATU protesting against government policy, tussles between NUM and the Chamber of Mines, and the odd altercation between sections of government and the platinum industry over black economic empowerment and social investment[53]—but with Marikana, a serious test, the bonds held firm.

In this case, the links are personified by Cyril Ramphosa, who, in addition to being a major figure in the ANC, owns 9.1 per cent of Lonmin.[54] In the Farlam Inquiry, Dali Mpofu, council for injured and arrested miners, summarised the contents of a series of damning emails involving Rampahosa. These included a warning to Mthethwa to come down hard on the strikers, and a recommendation to Susan Shabangu, Minister of Mineral Resources, that 'silence and inaction' on the events was 'bad for her and government'. Another headed 'Security Situation' read: 'You are absolutely correct in insisting that the minister [Shabangu] and indeed all government officials need to understand that we are essentially dealing with a criminal act. I have said as much to the minister of safety and security [presumably Minister of State Security, Siyabonga Cwele]'. He also advised leaders of NUM and planned to speak to Mantashe, ANC secretary general.[55] If these emails are substantiated, Rampahosa played a pivotal role in events, and the UK *Guardian* will have been vindicated in headlining its story with the phrase 'blood on his hands'.[56] Back In 1997, when Ramaphosa took over as Chair of Johnnic (obtaining a controlling interest from Anglo-American), Mark Gevisser wrote: 'The corporate sector is crowing. "Cyril Ramaphosa was the man who built the unions in the eighties," one very senior Anglo-American executive tells me, "and he'll be the one to break them in the nineties".[57] The trajectory was correct even if the timing was telescoped.

The main force underpinning the cohesion of the triangle and the main cause of the massacre were not immediate material interests, but an issue of principle. I refer to the labour relations regime—the means by which class antagonisms are managed through the institutionalisation of a balance of forces that existed at a particular moment in time. In practice, this is achieved through especially important laws, sometimes termed 'framing legislation'. Here, the key statute is the Labour Relations Act (LRA) of 1995, a relatively recent iteration of the Industrial Conciliation Act (ICA) of 1924, whose precepts have proved remarkably durable. The ICA, passed in the wake of the Rand Revolt and its defeat, introduced industrial councils that comprised unions and employers' associations within a specified industry. This was a corporatist arrangement whereby the unions disciplined workers and the employers' associations brought rogue capitalists into line. Employers were generally willing to deduct union dues from wages (the 'check-off') and strikes were prohibited for the duration of an agreement.[58] As Rob Davies argued, the act 'had the effect of bureaucratising the... trade unions (or at least of increasing the bureaucratisation already present).[59] The main limitation of the ICA was that, *de facto* and later *de jure*, African workers were excluded from the definition of 'employee', and thus from the benefits of the act. As a consequence of this racist provision, they tended to join separate black unions. The right for black workers to be included as employees was only won in 1979, following the Durban strikes of 1973 and the Soweto Uprising of 1976. The law was renamed the LRA in 1980, but the industrial councils and other major provisions of the ICA persisted.

However, the Act proved incapable of halting the insurrectionary workers' movement of the 1980s, which reached a peak in the miners' strike of 1987. The union, NUM, proposed 'a living wage' based on a 30 per cent increase in pay, but the employers refused to negotiate. For both sides, the battle was around something bigger—it was about 'control'! At its conference earlier in the year NUM had gone so far as to back a resolution calling for 'a democratic socialist society controlled by the working class'. Just as in 1922, the mine owners and police collaborated closely and the workers lost the strike. And, as in the aftermath of 1922, the employers acknowledged that long-term stability depended on compromise, and bit by bit they recognised the union, drawing it into bargaining structures established by the Chamber of Mines. Elsewhere, I have proposed that this outcome was a precursor to the political settlement of 1994.[60] Significantly, Ramaphosa led NUM in 1987 and led the ANC in the talks leading to 1994. Dunbar Moodie emphasises that '[w]hile Ramaphosa was willing to compromise on specifics... his commitment to worker self-respect... never wavered.'[61]

The amended LRA of 1995 had some new features, such as the establishment of the Commission for Conciliation, Mediation and Arbitration, but key characteristics of the old ICA remained intact (with industrial councils renamed 'bargaining councils'). In mining, there is industry-wide bargaining for gold and coal, but negotiations in platinum are company based. Unions with 50 per cent or more of the workers within a particular category can claim to represent all workers in that category, which is generally what happens. This practice, known as 'majoritarianism', is a barrier for smaller unions, and, when combined with the 'check-off', creates a basis for unions to be unresponsive to members' concerns. Leadership indifference reached its apogee in the mining industry, specifically at Lonmin. Thus, when

Marikana workers demanded to talk directly to their boss they were attacking the pivotal component of a labour regime that had worked to the advantage of union leaders and the companies alike.

On the same day that Lonmin workers won their pay hike, Baleni commented: 'The normal bargaining processes have been compromised. It does suggest that unprotected action, an element of anarchy, can be easily rewarded.'[62] Vavi, too, was alarmed, stating: 'We are not saying that workers do not deserve their money, but if we are not careful this may mean an end [to] the central bargaining system in the country. Workers will just embark on wildcat strikes and steam ahead, and force us [union leaders] to follow them.'[63] Shabangu pointed a finger at Impala, which, prior to the Lonmin conflict, had introduced two abnormal increases following a massive wildcat strike that ended in February 2012.[64] This, she argued, was a signal for unofficial action elsewhere. Again, she was raising the issue of threats to existing bargaining arrangements, from which NUM had benefitted.

The bigger problem

After Lonmin, workers at Angloplat came out in strike, encouraging the view that the platinum companies had created special problems for themselves, because, unlike the gold mines, they opposed centralised, industry-wide bargaining. However, rank-and-file strikes spread elsewhere: to the KDC mine owned by Goldfields, the world's fifth-largest gold producer; to mines operated by AngloGold Ashanti, the world's third-largest gold producer; to other gold mines; to a colliery and a diamond mine; to the very large and highly profitable Sishen iron ore mine (in which Anglo American has a majority stake); and to refineries and smelting plants linked to mines. In the process NUM was punished by mass defections to AMCU. This insurgency has fed a broader critique. Jay Naidoo, COSATU's first general secretary, and Hartford attacked majoritarianism, with the former arguing: 'When you recognise a union, but exclude it for the collective bargaining negotiations around the core issue of wages, you have a recipe for disaster.'[65] Hypothetically, the practice could be changed, but to what? In the present climate it is difficult to envisage a new model

Part of the workers' meeting on 18 August 2012, with Nkaneng informal settlement behind. A decision to continue the strike for R12,500 was agreed by acclaim.

that would be acceptable to all three of the major protagonists: the mine owners, NUM (and its powerful allies) and AMCU (under pressure from a new membership with high expectations)? AMCU is integrating new members, the Inquiry continues, NUM is suffering from shell shock and the ANC is divided by election fever, so no major change is imminent. More likely, there will be concessions on pay, some retrenchments and localised repression.

However, the labour relations regime cannot be wrenched apart from critical problems facing South African society as a whole. The post-Marikana crisis in the mining industry is part of a broader predicament facing the ANC, big business and union leaders, and it highlights the failure of the 1994 compromise. This is not the place to review literature on the subject, which is extensive, save to draw attention to recent valuable additions by Hein Marais and John Saul.[66] As underlined in a statement on Marikana signed by several hundred South African social scientists, continuities from the apartheid era are profound.[67] There are a few black capitalists, professional and skilled employees receive better pay, and there have been some improvements in social welfare, but for a large part of the population little has changed. The economy is still structured around a minerals-energy complex, it is still focused on export-led growth, and foreign capitalists repatriate their profits virtually unhindered.[68] Unemployment and inequality are worse than at the end of apartheid, and six in ten people of working age have no job of any kind. Even though mine workers are badly paid, median minimum wages are worse in other sectors.[69] The problem of low wages is compounded by the cost of caring for family members without incomes, and this combination pushes workers up against the labour relations' regime.

Since 2005, South Africa has probably experienced more strike days per capita than any other country.[70] The two largest were public-sector worker strikes held in 2007 and 2010, with the second of these entailing greater rank-and-file participation.[71] More broadly, the *Workers Survey* revealed that 'around half of COSATU members involved in a strike thought that violence was necessary', with most of the violence, or threats of violence, being directed at scabs.[72] In addition, South Africa's level of ongoing urban unrest is greater than anywhere else in the world, and there were more community protests in the first six months of 2012 than in any previous year.[73] The working class gained confidence from the critical part it played in the overthrow of apartheid, and it has been accumulating grievances without suffering major defeats in the post-apartheid period. This is a dangerous moment for the country's rulers, and it is more difficult to reform the labour relations' regime now than it was in 1924, 1979 or 1985. No doubt there will also be some in the cabinet who will recall Alexis de Tocqueville's aphorism that 'the most dangerous moment for a bad government is when it begins to reform'.

On the workers' side

Putting matters simply, a massacre occurred because the police killed striking mineworkers, but it also happened because the strikers refused to be intimidated. They knew in advance that they might be killed, but they stayed on the mountain. *Why did they do so?* Available studies by labour historians are particularly strong on pre-existing solidarities and they pose valuable questions for the further investigation that is necessary.[74] Our own research is merely suggestive at this stage. We know that most Lonmin workers were oscillating male migrants from Pondoland, and that RDOs from Karee took the lead, but what is the significance of these demographics and occupational categories? Were they fundamental in some way, or does their salience lie in the way they were associated with alienation from NUM? In searching for explanations of this remarkable resilience we should not underestimate the significance of the preceding days of struggles and nights on the mountain, or miss the importance of friendships and close family ties (which sometimes determined who was with whom as the tension mounted and the killing started). Clearly, pay was the central issue, not only because it affected funds available for remittances, food and so on, but also, perhaps, because of its relationship to intensity of work and to health and safety. It is clear that management's refusal to talk was a crunch issue. But what was that about? Is it too fanciful to think that it concerned something that Ramaphosa once understood: 'worker self-respect'?

Following the Lonmin victory, strikes spread like wild fire, raising new possibilities for workers. The first lesson was that NUM was an encumbrance, and the second was that strike committees could unite workers. Before long there were attempts to co-ordinate the strikes, and on 19 September a statement was issued in the name of the Rustenburg Joint Strike Co-ordinating Committee. This applauded the Lonmin victory, stating that it had inspired them to continue their fight, and that the 'framework of negotiations, [which exists] above the heads and behind the backs of us, has been torn down'. It concluded by raising a number of demands that included: a living wage; an end to the [unofficial] state of emergency; re-employment of sacked workers; nationalisation of the mines under democratic control of workers and communities; decent housing, basic services and education; and work for all.[75] The Rustenburg committee invited participation from outside its area, and at least 70 people attended a National Strike Co-ordinating Committee meeting held on 13

October. These included representatives from the striking gold mines in the Carltonville district. Workers have now returned to work, and the movement has waned, but worker organisation on the mines will never be the same again. Thousands of workers have rejected their old union and many of these have linked strike mobilisation to politics in a new way.

It is likely that in the Rustenburg mining district, the largest in the country, most workers have joined AMCU or will do so in the near future, and the union will make substantial headway elsewhere. AMCU has two major advantages for workers. First, from engagement with the union's leaders, it appears to be more committed to democratic decision making than NUM, and, at least to start with, will respond positively to the demands of its members. Secondly, it does not carry the burden of an alliance with the governing party. However, there are challenges too. The first of these is that NUM's separation from ordinary workers was not only a consequence of lack of accountability, it was also material, and AMCU will have to review inherited practices, including the payment of C_1 salaries to senior stewards. The second is that, in rejecting political affiliation, AMCU should not reject political participation. In the 1980s unions affiliated to the Federation of South African Trade Unions generally abstained from politics (a form of 'workerism'), creating a vacuum that was filled by unions aligned to the ANC (a form of 'populism'), thus paving the way to the ruling party's dominance among workers. Most issues raised by the Rustenburg Committee, for instance, require an engagement with politics, and if AMCU does not provide this, workers are likely to be drawn in other directions, perhaps even back towards NUM. The union cannot duck the question of ownership of the mines because this has a direct bearing on the quality of life of mineworkers and their communities (including key issues such as a living wage, intensity of work, health and safety, housing, and access to land). Given the negative experiences that South Africans have had with state-run industries in the recent past, some scepticism about nationalisation is understandable. This could benefit just a few people, but it could also be done differently; perhaps, quoting the NUM's 1987 resolution, on

Marikana workers celebrate their victory at Wonderkop Stadium on 18 September 2012.

the basis of 'a democratic socialist society controlled by the working class'.

The desires promoted in the Rustenburg statement can only be attained on the basis of organising beyond mining—in other industries, among students, and in the communities. The reason for this is partly organisational, but it is also political—the need to counter the dominant ideas in society, including those of the ANC and SACP. Immediately after the massacre, the ANC Youth League and its former president, Julius Malema, provided Marikana workers with valuable moral and practical support, and Malema's speeches on various other mines probably contributed to expansion of the strike movement.[76] However, this input has not been sustained, perhaps because of election battles within the ANC and as a consequence of corruption and tax-avoidance charges laid against Malema. Two socialist organisations have also come to the fore. One is the Democratic Socialist Movement (DSM), which includes Mametlwe Sebei, who acted as the Angloplat workers' spokesperson for a while. The other is the Democratic Left Front (DLF), whose members include Rehad Desai, co-ordinator of the Marikana Support Campaign. While the DSM is an old-style socialist group, the DLF, the more substantial of the two, is a 'point of convergence' that involves community associations alongside individual activists and smaller political groupings. The emergence of these organisations is further evidence that ANC/SACP hegemony is now being challenged from the left.

A final word

The Marikana Massacre was ghastly. In other settings, events of this kind have led to the defeat of a movement, or at least its abeyance. But that is not what happened here. On the contrary, the strike got stronger. Workers faced trauma, the tribulations of burying their dead in far-away places, threatened sackings, lack of money for food, and attacks from unions and politicians. But, by 7 September the company was reporting that attendance at work was down to two per cent, and after that it gave up providing statistics. There was an undeclared state of emergency and a community leader was killed, but still the workers fought on, until, on 18 September, they agreed to a settlement that secured them victory. Had the strike collapsed, people across the country fighting poverty and injustice would have been cowed. The opposite happened and, from the perspective of the state and the bosses, the killings were an appalling miscalculation, an enormous setback. Somehow, despite 34 colleagues being killed and with many more injured or detained, workers found the strength to pull themselves together and determine that the strike would continue. This was one of the most remarkable acts of courage in labour history, anywhere and at any time.

Notes

1   The Truth and Reconciliation Commission, *Bisho Massacre*, downloaded from www.justice.gov.za/trc; Staff Reporters, 'Boipatong: still no real answers'. *Mail & Guardian*, 6 October 2000.

2   Sifiso Mxolisi Ndlovu, *The Soweto Uprising: Counter-memories of June 1976* (Ravan Press, Press, 1998); Philip Bonner and Lauren Segal, *Soweto: A History* (Maskew Miller, Cape Town).

3   Jeremy Krikler, *The Rand Revolt: The 1922 Insurrection and Racial Killing in South Africa* (Jonathan Ball, Johannesburg, 2005).

4   I am indebted to Duncan for these findings, which were contained in an email dated 19 September. In descending order, the remaining categories included: other—13%, parliament/political parties—10%, government—9%, independent experts—8%, NUM—6%, police—5%, and AMCU –5%.

5   Jane Duncan, 'Media underplaying police, state brutality', *Sunday Independent*, 26 August 2012.

6   Thapelo Lekgowa, Botsang Mmope and Peter Alexander, 'Geography of a massacre', *Socialist Worker*, 21 August 2012; Khadija Patel, 'Marikana: What really happened?' *Daily Maverick*, 23 August 2012; Greg Marinovich, 'The Murder Fields of Marikana', *Daily Maverick*, 30 August 2012. The last of these articles was reproduced in the *Mail & Guardian* on 31 August 2012.

7   Reuters, 'Two killed in union violence at Lonmin mine', 13 August 2012, disseminated by *Mail & Guardian* online; Rahima Essop and Stephen Grootes, 'Police must do more at Lonmin', *Eyewitness News*, 13 August 2012; 'Mines minister Shabangu ready to intervene to stop Lonmin violence', *SA Labour News*, 15 August 2012.

8   Frans Baleni, 'State probe must reveal the real force behind the mine tragedy', *Sunday Independent*, 26 August 2012.

9   Sibongakonke Shoba and Isaac Mahlangu, 'Muti "protected" miners', *Sunday Times*, 19 August 2012. This item was responsible for a third of the 'worker' sources counted by Duncan (see above). Of these, two were 'locals' rather than strikers, and the other two, who had been on the mountain, failed to confirm the story.

10   See, for instance, T. Dunbar Moodie, 'Becoming a social movement union: Cyril Ramaphosa and the National Union of Mineworkers', *Transformation* 72/73 (2010), pp 153–4. Moodie tells the story of Lira Setona, a miners' leader, who made use of muti. When Setona's 'sidekick' was asked about the muti, he laughed and commented: 'No. It was holy water that protected him [i.e. Setona]'. Moodie adds: 'Muti by another name, I thought.'

11   In the Inquiry, the SAPS has used the sangoma argument as part of its defence. Bishop Jo Seoka, chair of the South African Council of Churches, responded by telling the Commission: 'Allegations that muti was protecting workers against bullets, it's stupid, it's nonsense, you're making black people stupid.' Lucas Ledwaba, 'Shadow of Man in the Green Blanket', *City Press*, 18 November 2012.

12   Ralph Darlington, '"Agitator theory" of strikes re-evaluated', *Labor History* 47(4) (2006).

13   Lebogang Seale, Baldwin Ndaba, Poloko Tau and Solly Maphumulo, 'A Nation Seethes', The Star, 20 August 2012; David Bruce, 'The truth about Marikana', *Sunday Times Review*, 9 September 2012.

14   South African Police Service, 'Media Statement: General Phiyega Pronounces on Mine Unrest', 17 August 2012.

15   Ibid; Dennis Adriao, police spokesperson quoted in *SA Labour News*, 17 August 2012.

16 Republic of South Africa, *Constitution*, Chapter Two: Bill of Rights, available at http://www.info.gov.za/documents/constitution.

17 Niren Tolsi, 'Miners killed like "possessed vermin" says lawyer', *Mail & Guardian*, online, 22 October 2012.

18 These were the Special Task Force, National Intervention Unit and Tactical Response Teams, all grouped under SAPS's Operational Response Services, which also includes public order units. David Bruce, 'The Road to Marikana: Abuses of Force During Public Order Policing Operations', *South African Civil Society Information Service*, 12 October 2012.

19 Poloko Tau, 'Marikana Riddle', *The Star*, 6 November 2012.

20 Tolsi, ibid.

21 John Mkize, 'Marikana: Bodies seen on the ground', *Business Report*, 16 August 2012.

22 On 16 August there were 630 police officers on day shift and 88 on night shift in Marikana. *Time Live*, 'Marikana inquiry updates 8 November 2012', downloaded from www.timeslive.co.za on 19 November 2012.

23 Ronnie Kasrils, 'It was like poking a hornet's nest', *Sunday Times*, 26 August 2012. My emphasis.

24 Louise Flanagan, 'Now police go shopping for pepper spray, shields', *The Star*, 17 October 2012.

25 Report on media briefing by General Phiyega, *News24*, 17 August 2012, and *Sowetan Live*, 17 August 2012.

26 Staff reporters, 'Lonmin: Questions for Zuma', *City Press*, 19 August 2012. Marikana inquiry updates.

27 Immediately after the massacre Mthethwa told Lonmin not to sack their workers (out of respect for the state's week of mourning), and had he adopted a similarly firm stance in the week leading to the 16th, telling the employer to talk with the strikers, deaths would have been averted. See SAPA and *Mail & Guardian* Online reporter, 'Mthethwa tells Lonmin to dial down threat to fire Marikana strikers', *Mail & Guardian* Online, 21 August 2012.

28 Bench Marks Foundation, *Communities in the Platinum Minefields* (Bench Marks Foundation, Johannesburg, 2012), pp 73, 81.

29 Michele Taal, Saliem Patel and Trenton Elsley, 'A mineworker's wage: the only argument against the R12,500 is greed,' Labour Research Services, 28 August 2012, and see *Amandla* 26/27, September 2012. For the year ending 30 September 2011, Lonmin made $1.549 million after payments for materials and services. 51.8 per cent of this went to 'salaries and benefits'. 2.4 per cent went to directors and shareholders. A further 43.1 per cent went to 'cash retained for sustainable growth'; that is, investment in future profits. Workers were subsidising new investments on a massive scale, and it was not too difficult for Lonmin to channel some of this cash back to workers in the form of increased pay. Lonmin Plc, *Building for the Future* (Lonmin Plc, London, 2011), p. 55.

30 Jo Seoka, 'Charges against miners raise questions', *Business Day*, 5 September 2012. Emphasis added.

31 Gia Nicolaides, 'Two cops killed in Lonmin violence', *Eyewitness News*, 13

August 2012. Later, the Inquiry heard that hand-written posters demanding R12 500 had appeared at Karee as early as June. Kwanele Sosibo, 'Lonmin cut deal with rock drillers', *Mail & Guardian*, 7 December 2012.

32   Malcolm Rees, 'Lonmin death toll at 34, 78 injured', *Money Web*, 16 August 2012.

33   Frans Baleni and Lesiba Seshoka, 'NUM calls for a Special Task Force in the mines', *COSATU Today*, downloaded from www.cosatu.org.za/docs/cosatu2day/2012/pro813a on 31 October 2012. Emphasis added.

34   See Baleni on YouTube, www.youtube.com/watch?v=bDU71-rJkY, downloaded on 5 October 2012.

35   Frans Baleni, 'State probe must reveal the real force behind the mine tragedy', *Sunday Independent*, 26 August 2012.

36   COSATU, *Secretariat Political Report if the 11th National Congress* (COSATU, Johannesburg, 2012), p 33.

37   Matuma Letsoalo, 'Uproar over unionist's huge salary hike just "a campaign"', *Mail & Guardian* Online, 18 May 2012.

38   Gavin Hartford, 'Alienation, paucity and despair', *Mail & Guardian*, 12 October 2012. The reference to shop stewards should be qualified. Hartford is referring to senior stewards, branch leaders, who are paid at the level of personnel officers, and ordinary shaft stewards have far fewer perks. See Andries Bezuidenhout and Sakhela Buhlungu, 'Old Victories, New Struggles: the State of the National Union of Mineworkers.' In Sakhela Buhlungu, John Daniel, Roger Southall and Jessica Latchman, *State of the Nation: South Africa 2007* (HSRC Press, Cape Town, 2007), p. 251.

39   For Ramaphosa, see Anthony Butler, *Cyril Ramaphosa* (Jacana Media, Johannesburg, 2007). For Motlanthe, see Ebrahim Harvey, *Kgalema Motlanthe: A Political Biography* (Jacana Media, Johannesburg, 2012).

40   See Bezuidenhout and Buhlungu, ibid, p. 250–1.

41   Timothy Sizwe Phakathi, 'Worker agency in colonial, apartheid and post-apartheid gold mining workplace regimes', *Review of African Political Economy* 39(132) (2008), pp 279–294.

42   Sakhela Buhlungu and Andries Bezuidenhout, 'Union Solidarity under Stress: the case of the National Union of Mineworkers in South Africa.' *Labour Studies Journal* 33(3) (2008), pp 262–287.

43   COSATU, *Workers Survey* (Johanneburg, COSATU, 2012), p. 37.

44   Bezuidenhout and Buhlungu, Old Victories, p. 252.

45   COSATU, 'COSATU's 11th Congress Declaration on the Lonmin Marikana platinum mine tragedy, the mining industry, and general poverty wages, as adopted with amendments 17th September 2012.' Against the prevailing position, the National Union of Metalworkers of South Africa (NUMSA) 'condemned the intransigence and insensitivity of the mine bosses... and the savage, cowardly actions and excessive force used by the police, which invariably [sic] led to the... the police massacre of 34 [workers].' See NUMSA, statement on 'The Marikana Massacre', 'NUMSA Central Committee (CC) Press Statement' dated 2 September 2012. In contrast to COSATU, AMCU's

federation, the National Council of Trade Unions (NACTU), denounced 'the brutal massacre of miners by the police who acted upon high level orders from ANC government.' See Narius Moloto, 'NACTU Press Statement on the recent development on Lonmin Marikana', 18 September 2012.

46 COSATU, Secretariat Political Report, p. 33.

47 Blade Nzimande, 'Defend the gains of the working class. Take responsibility for the national democratic revolution', speech distributed at the 11th COSATU Congress.

48 Olebogeng Molatilwa, 'Report takes swipe at state, unions and mining bosses', Sowetan, 7 September 2012.

49 Hartford, 'Alienation, paucity and despair'.

50 Goldfields spokesperson interviewed on SAfm at about 07:30 on 21 September 2012.

51 Author's notes on COSATU Congress.

52 According to the Sunday Times rich list, Motsepe was the most wealthy South African in 2011, but slipped to fourth place in 2012 (he was still worth R20.1 billion though). Radebe's department withdrew support for families of slain Marikana miners wishing to attend the Farlam Inquiry. Jana Marais, 'Rich still in pound seats', Sunday Times, 16 September 2012; News24, Marikana families lose travel funding.

53 See Gavin Capps, 'A bourgeois reform with social justice? The contradictions of the Minerals Development Bill and black economic empowerment in the South African platinum industry', Review of Political Economy 39(132).

54 Lloyd Gedye, 'The ANC's prodigal son returns', Mail & Guardian, 2 November 2012. In 2011 Ramaphosa received R680,000 in director's fees. Jacques Pauw and Thanduxolo Jika, 'The great R1.2m divide', City Press, 26 August 2012. Ramaphosa is Chair of the ANC's national disciplinary committee of appeals, and is being touted as a possible deputy president of the party (and hence, in all likelihood, the country).

55 Graeme Hoskins, 'Marikana inquiry shown Ramapahosa emails,' The Times, 24 October 2012, downloaded from Sowetan Live.

56 David Smith, 'Ramaphosa has blood on his hands, say miners,' The Guardian, 25 October 2012.

57 Mark Gevisser, 'Ending Economic Apartheid: South Africa's New Captains of Industry', The Nation, 29 September 1997, p. 24, quoted in John S. Saul, The Next Liberation Struggle: Capitalism, Socialism and Democracy in Southern Africa (UKZN Press, Scottsville, 2005), pp 211–12.

58 Peter Alexander, Workers, War and the Origins of Apartheid: Labour and Politics in South Africa, 1939-'48, James Currey, Oxford, 2000), p. 11.

59 Robert H. Davies, Capital, State and White Labour in South Africa 1900– 1960: An Historical Materialist Analysis of Class Formation and Class Relations (Harvester, Brighton, 1979), p. 195.

60 Peter Alexander, 'South Africa's Great Miners' Strike of 1987: Towards a Re-examination', Proceedings of the Sixth International Mining History Conference, Akabira City, Hokkaido, Japan, 18 (2003).

61 T. Dunbar Moodie, 'Managing the 1987 Mine Workers' Strike', *Journal of Southern African Studies* 35(1) (2009), p. 51. See also, T. Dunbar Moodie, 'Comprehending Class Compromise in the History of Class Struggle on the South African Gold Mines: Variations and Vicissitudes of Class Power,' *South African Review of Sociology* 41(3) (2010).

62 AFP, 'S. African union warns Lonmin deal "rewards anarchy"', AFP, 19 September 2012.

63 Ranjeni Munusamy, 'Cosatu at the crossroads', *New Age*, 21 September 2012.

64 Allan Seccombe and Natasha Marrian, 'Shabangu blames Implats for spreading strikes', *Business Day*, 3 October 2012. On the Implats strike, see Crispin Chinguno, 'Impala Platinum Strike: Lessons and Implications', *South African Labour Bulletin* 36(2), August 2012; Trevor Ngwane and Botsang Mmope, 'Impala strike linking workplace with community struggles', *South African Labour Bulletin* 36(2), August 2012. When we asked our reference group about Impala, they denied its significance for their own struggle.

65 Jay Naidoo, 'Marikana: the aftermath,' *City Press*, 26 August 2012; Hartford, Alienation, paucity and despair.

66 Hein Marais, *South Africa Pushed to the Limit: the Political Economy of Change* (UCT Press, Cape Town, 2011); John S. Saul, 'The transition in South Africa: choice, fate... or recolonisation?' Critical Arts 26(4) (2012).

67 'Marikana: Statement by South African Social Scientists', http://marikanastatement.blogspot.com.

68 Sam Ashman, Ben Fine and Susan Newman, 'Amnesty International? The Nature, Scale and Impact of Capital Flight from South Africa', *Journal of Southern African Studies* 37(1) (2011). For the political economy of platinum see Gavin Capps, 'Victim of its own success? The platinum mining industry and the apartheid mineral property system in South Africa's political transition', *Review of African Political Economy* 39(131) (2012).

69 Taal, Patel and Elsley, A mineworker's wage, p. 3.

70 Peter Alexander, 'Barricades, ballots and experimentation: making sense of the 2011 local government election with a social movement lens'. In Marcelle C. Dawson and Luke Sinwell, *Contesting Transformation: Popular Resistance in Twenty-first Century South Africa* (Pluto Press, London, 2012).

71 Claire Ceruti, 'The hidden element in the 2010 public-sector strike in South Africa', *Review of African Political Economy* 38(117) (2011).

72 COSATU, Workers Survey, p. 23. The report continued: 'Around two in five thought that violence by the police or management was an appropriate response to the strikers' behaviour'.

73 Lonmin complained that community unrest had 'several times' led to loss of production during the first half of 2012. These disturbances, they said, were 'a result of high unemployment and poverty'. Lonmin Plc, '2012 Interim Results Announcement', 14 May 2012, pp 9, 12.

74 The key texts are T. Dunbar Moodie with Vivienne Ndatshe, *Going for Gold: Men, Mines and Migration* (University of California Press, Berkeley, 1994) and the three volumes of Vic Allen's *The History of Black Mineworkers in South*

Africa. See also William Beinart's work on Pondoland and amaPondo migrants; Peter Alexander, 'Oscillating Migrants, "Detribalised Families" and Militancy: Mozambicans on Witbank Collieries, 1918–1927', *Journal of Southern African Studies* 27(3) (2001); Eddy Tshidiso Maloka, *Basotho and the Mines: A Social History of Labour Migrancy in Lesotho and South Africa* (CODESRIA, Dakar, 2004); Dhiraj Nite and Paul Stewart (eds), *Mining Faces: An Oral History of Work in Gold and Coal Mines in South Africa: 1951-2011* (Jacana Media, Johannesburg, 2012).

75 The statement appears on pp 3–5 of Maria van Driel (ed), *Documents of the Social Movements 2012. Special Edition: Marikana* (Khanya Publishing, Johannesburg, 2012).

76 The following exchange in the back of our car provides an interpretation of the relationship between Malema and the strikers. Fieldworker: 'Do you think Malema would have supported you if he was still president of the Youth League?' Worker: 'No.' Fieldworker: 'So he was being an opportunist?' Worker: 'Yes.' Fieldworker: 'So why did you let him use you?' Worker: 'Because we were using him.'

They died at Marikana

Name	Date of birth	Place of burial
Andries Motlapula Ntshenyeho* [N]	15 June 1970	Harry Gwala Section, Vereeniging, GP
Anele Mdizeni*	6 February 1983	Desi Location, Elliotdale, EC
Babalo Mtshazi*	25 February 1986	Njilo Location, Libode, EC
Bongani Mdze*	5 May 1984	Hantshudu Village, Matatiele, EC
Bongani Nqongophele*	27 September 1981	Kwaleni Village, Elliotdale, EC
Bonginkosi Yona* [N]	6 December 1980	Magashu Village, Lady Frere, EC
Cebisile Yawa*	5 July 1988	Mthingwevu Village, Cala, EC
Fezile David Saphendu*	24 December 1988	Cawu Location, Mqanduli, EC
Hassan Duncan Fundi [S] [N]	11 June 1965	Rustenburg, NW
Hendrick Tsietsi Monene [P]	1 April 1965	Ekangala, Tshwane, GP
Isaiah Twala [N]	18 January 1961	Not known
Jackson Lehupa*	8 May 1964	Bethania, Mount Fletcher, EC
Janeveke Raphael Liau*	14 September 1967	Likolobeng, Lesotho
John Kutlwano 'Papi' Ledingoane*	22 April 1988	Wonderkop, NW
Julius Tokoti Mancotywa*	30 March 1951	Sterkspruit, Herschel, EC
Khanare Elias Monesa*	21 January 1976	Boroeng, Buthe Buthe, Lesotho
Mafolisi Mabiya*	20 November 1983	Msegethi Village, Idutywa, EC

Makhosandile Mkhonjwa*	20 February 1983	KwaMadiba Village, Bizana, EC
Matlhomola Mabelane [S]	6 November 1964	Damsonville, Brits, NW
Mgcineni 'Mambush' Noki*	2 February 1982	Thwalikhulu Village, Mqanduli, EC
Michael Ngweyi*	3 March 1973	Mvezo Villa, Mbashe Bridge, Mthatha, EC
Modisaotsile Van Wyk Sagalala* [N]	2 July 1952	Nkaneng, Wonderkop, NW
Molefi Osiel Ntsoele* [N]	1 January 1972	Semonkong, Lesotho
Mongezeleli Ntenetya* [N]	9 June 1978	Falakhle Village, Dutywa, EC
Mphangeli Thukuza*	16 November 1970	Quba, Ngqeleni, EC
Mpumzeni Ngxande*	22 June 1974	Lujizweni, Ngqeleni, EC
Mvuyisi Henry Pato* [N]	13 November 1977	Mbobeni Village, Bizana, EC
Mzukisi Sompeta*	3 January 1976	Phumlo Area, Lusikisiki, EC
Nkosiyabo Xalabile*	11 March 1982	Desi Location, Elliotdale, EC
Nkumbulo Mvume	9 October 1983	Gxulu, Zithathele, Libode, EC
Nobhozi Bhabhazela	6 May 1954	Thuku Location, Gqubeni, Mqanduli, EC
Ntandazo Nokamba* [N]	6 January 1976	Ncolora Village, Libode, EC
Patrick Akhona Jijase*	12 March 1986	Dwaku Village, Ntabankulu, EC

Pumzile Sokanyile	21 May 1964	Mdumazulu Location, Ngqeleni, EC
Sello Lepaaku [P]	23 January 1967	Seabe, Siyabuswa, MP
Semi Jokanisi	25 December 1982	Hombe Village, Lusikisiki, EC
Stelega Gadlela*	1 January 1962	Manzini, Swaziland
Telang Vitalis Mohai*	6 October 1975	Maseru, Lesotho
Thapelo Eric Mabebe	9 June 1975	Not known
Thobile Mpumza*	6 July 1986	Gugwini Village, Mount Ayliff, EC
Thabiso Johannes Thelejane*	30 October 1955	Paballong Village, Matatiele, EC
Thabiso Mosebetsane* [N]	7 February 1963	Matsheleng Village, Matatiele, EC
Thembinkosi Gwelani*	6 July 1985	Makhwalweni Location, Lusikisiki, EC
Thembalakhe Sabelo Mati [N]	10 October 1963	Kundile Village, Ntabankulu, EC
Thobisile Zibambele	10 September 1973	KwaBala Village, Goqwana, Lusikisiki, EC

* = died on 16 August; [N] = NUM member; [P] = police; [S] = security guard; EC = Eastern Cape; GP = Gauteng; NW = Northwest; MP = Mpumalanga.

Sources: Lonmin Plc; South African Funeral Practitioners Association; *The Star*, 23 August 2012; *New Age*, 8 November 2012; *Eyewitness News*, 16 August 2012; *Mail & Guardian*, 7 September 2012, *City Press* Face of Marikana Project.

Note: This table includes 45 names. Isaiah Twala appears on some but not all lists. There is a question mark over the date on which Semi Jokanisi died.